Co...

of

Love

By
R C Liston

MAPLE
PUBLISHERS

Colours of Love

Author: R C Liston

Copyright © R C Liston (2023)

First Published in 2023

ISBN 978-1-915796-88-2 (Paperback)
         978-1-915796-89-9 (Hardback)
         978-1-915796-90-5 (eBook)

Book cover design and Book layout by:

   White Magic Studios
   www.whitemagicstudios.co.uk

Published by:

   Maple Publishers
   Fairbourne Drive, Atterbury,
   Milton Keynes,
   MK10 9RG, UK
   www.maplepublishers.com

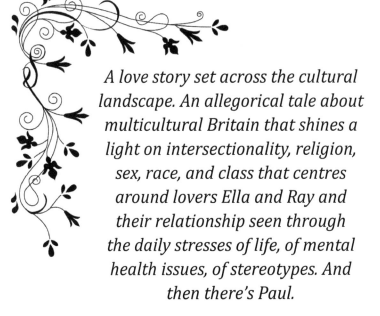

A love story set across the cultural landscape. An allegorical tale about multicultural Britain that shines a light on intersectionality, religion, sex, race, and class that centres around lovers Ella and Ray and their relationship seen through the daily stresses of life, of mental health issues, of stereotypes. And then there's Paul.

Contents

Prologue

I often wonder what became of Paul. His disappearance more than a year ago still bothers me because I cannot help feeling a sense of responsibility for what happened to Ray's best friend. He just vanished; his presence erased. Is he dead? Somehow it feels like it. I can't help feeling that it was all my fault. Was Paul killed because of what happened? Has he moved away - to Europe or America, perhaps the Caribbean where he might have adopted a new identity? No one really knows. Ray and I plan to get married and while I am excited about the prospect of becoming Mrs Ella Gordon, and finally getting rid of the cumbersome Somerton-Hughes surname that I have had to drag around with me all my life like an anvil around my neck, I cannot filter out the memories of Paul, no matter how hard I try. But I must try - for the sake of my marriage, for the sake of my mental health and not least, for the sake of Ray's wellbeing. They were best friends, but that relationship untangled quicker than a ball of wool. I never understood why - until much later.

My name is Ella Somerton-Hughes. I don't know why my parents decided that it was at all ok to combine their surnames. Apart from being a mouthful for everyone, it sends a signal of privilege, it shouts privilege, a situation that I was not happy about as I was growing up. I didn't like having my social status broadcast to all and sundry without me having any say in the matter, and particularly at a time when I began to understand the subtle connotations of what that perceived privilege might look like to some. Marrying Ray would, at last, make things more precise, neater at least. "Gordon" I like the sound of that. Easy to tease into a signature, easy to remember, and easy, too, for the children - when they come along, if they come along. Let's not take things for granted.

Paul, though, remains an answer that until now, has eluded all questions. While I was not a particular friend, Paul chose the option to do bad things when all available avenues were there for him to do good things. But that's all behind me, behind us, I can't exclude Ray in how all this has played out. However, I should really focus on my wedding and Ray's and my future together, rather than worry about that sordid episode, which, in reality, is probably best forgotten anyway. Let sleeping dogs lie. But the trouble is, the dogs won't sleep; there remains an occasional growl that jumps up and becomes a sharp bite whenever the question of what happened to Paul comes up, as it does from time to time. But more importantly, he was Ray's best friend. I do wonder how what happened to him has affected Ray.

As I fidget in the bridal shop in Greenwich, it is clear from my demeanour that my mind is not on the dress fitting, which only makes the job of the increasingly agitated shop assistant, who has been patient to a fault, despite what must seem to him as this irritating, half-interested would-be bride, much harder. OK, focus. Do I go for an A-line dress? No, that might not suit my figure. Or should I opt for a puffy merengue with a fitted bodice with a dramatic, full skirt. Maybe that's too princess-like, too traditional. Or should I go for a simple shift dress? I'm glad Rebecca is here for a second opinion, but I think a shift style elongates my torso and draws attention to my waist. I like it but I can't make up my mind. But the poor chap attending me has no idea what is causing my thoughts to be performing somersaults at a time when I should be totally engaged with the process and showing an excited grin to the world, a state of euphoria that I assume every bride-to-be exhibits. But given the situation that I find myself in, I should be able to put any thought of Paul out of my mind, but I can't. He remains an irritating itch that needs to be scratched. I can't shake the uncertainty, the doubts, the questions - if the right decisions were made by the right people at the right time. I suppose we will never know. I suppose Paul will never know - wherever he is.

But all that is history. My history, Ray's history and not least, Paul's history. I want to silence the cacophony that is ringing in my ear. Constantly! Marriage is a time to look ahead, look to the future and a new beginning, a life that does not include old, unwanted memories that hang around. Getting married is when you dust off what has gone before, polish the new and write your own happy future.

Genesis

The sumptuous, long flirtatious summer meanders by as wistfully as a thought. It embraces you, teases you, fills you with promises, laughs with you and then laughs in your face. It fills you to bursting with eager excitement and longing and in a fleeting moment it rolls over, spent and makes way for sober autumn. Summer mornings have a skill of washing over you like a dose of dopamine, the difference with summers as opposed to spring, autumn or winter, is the lack of crisp uncertainty in the air. Summers offer up the promise a mix of what the day has in store, the clarity and energy with which the welcome warmth, the mottled sunlight and the smell of fresh flowers entice. Ray woke up counting down the hours before Monday morning and work, while at the same time wishing that they wouldn't come. It's one of life's inevitabilities: that Monday-morning feeling, the grating battle with other commuters for a seat on the 07:15; for the wish that the sweaty bearded man who always nudged his way to the same spot every morning would, for the sake of the rest of us, invest in better personal hygiene; for the vacant faces, all bar none, would one day strike up a conversation, if only to extend a cheery good morning greeting.

But this was Sunday morning, no work, no pushing and shoving and no negotiating the space between fellow commuters - and Ray was going to lap it up, savouring the last vestiges of the weekend.

The smell of the rich brew of deep-roasted Arabica made from Ella's unnecessarily expensive coffee maker drifted from the kitchen to the tray that was now perched on the bedside table in her bedroom. It was an aroma that tangled with Ray's senses, forcing his barely awake self to breathe in. At that moment Ella walked in carrying fruits and croissants; the morning sunlight highlighting her uncombed paprika-hued hair that reminded Ray of the colour of rusted autumn leaves, her voluptuous curves a gossamer outline under her flimsy nightdress. It wasn't Ella's natural hair colour but a shade she adopted after discovering that Rita Hayworth, her favourite film star from a period when Hollywood really had stars, had a flowing mess of red hair.

That same sunlight penetrated her flimsy-thin oversized sleepwear and ebbed and flowed over her firm figure, outlining her nipples standing erect as if they were eager puppies full of play and willing to please.

Ray loved these moments, watching, staring, and drinking in before savouring every inch, every move, every twist of Ella's swaying hips. Ray pondered, pointlessly in that blokish way, whether she was up for it. "Ray, your coffee's ready," Ella said nonchalantly interrupting her boyfriend's lascivious thoughts, "and the papers are in there," she added, pointing to the small kitchen that could be seen from her bedroom, a cosy space that was carefully decorated in neutral colours with complementary accented touches that reflected her personality. Oh, to be loved, Ray thought to himself.

The sight of his girlfriend sashaying around her flat gave rise to Ray's racy side. Ella's movement set off a cascade of reminiscing about the first time they made love, how nervous yet how excited he was. The tingling feeling that he had now was the same as that first time. The only difference was that then their relationship was new, and he was getting to know Ella. On this Sunday morning, though, the faltering, uncertain steps that every new couple must take were no more. Those doubt-filled moments and pregnant pauses were no more, replaced with a jaunty confidence that only comes with time and familiarity.

Ray recalled how the anticipation of sex was in itself a turn on. After their relationship took a more serious turn, the couple enjoyed a full sex life. The deeper, more intimate side of their relationship started after Ray and Ella had been dining at a newly opened restaurant chosen by Ella, who wanted to sample the traditional Jordanian cuisine that was on offer at the eatery.

"What do you look for in a woman, Ray?" Ella asked between mouthfuls of falafel.

"A sense of humour, fun... you know, the usual. What I don't like in a woman, or at least what I find unattractive, is someone who takes themselves too seriously and takes life too seriously. Life is tough enough as it is, therefore, I believe that we should always view things sunny side up, the glass half full."

"That's all well and good, Ray, but it's not really what I am asking. What I want to know is what are the physical attributes that turn you on, the things that make you want more. More cuddles, more long caresses, more soft kisses, and then even more soft kisses, and more.... Well, you know what I mean. For example, I like it when a man takes control in bed. I find it especially sexy when I am dominated. I like to give in to my desires and allow my passion to flow. I like to be kissed softly - all over, then teased, I like to nibble at the hors d'oeuvres before moving on to the main course. But I will reciprocate, I like to have my turn in the driving seat, I also like to control as well as being told what to do. Yes, I like doing the things that I like to do."

"Such as?"

"You'll have to wait and see," Ella said with a grin.

"Is that a promise?"

"You'll have to wait and see. And if that promise is fulfilled, what will you do to me?"

"You'll have to wait and see Ella," came Ray's reply.

"I don't think I can wait," replied Ella excitedly.

The flirtation continued between the couple through the main course and mouthfuls of muhallabia, a flirtation that was further fuelled by wine and heated anticipation that was infused with a growing longing to be in each other's arms. It was a moment in time when it was clear that their new relationship was about to be progressed to the next level.

Ella placed the key into the lock of her heavy oak front door, but held back, gripping the door before fully opening it. She turned to Ray and whispered seductively in his ear, "I may not let you in unless you promise me that you'll be a very bad boy. Will you be gentle, or will you take me in a heated rush? What type of lover are you, Ray?" It did not take long before Ella's question was answered. Ray pushed the heavy door open, scooped Ella up in his arms and kissed her fully. She felt Ray's urgency and flung her arms around him in wanton enthusiasm. He responded with eager kisses, she opened herself to the possibility of being loved how she wanted to be: softly, passionately, and enthusiastically. Their desire for each other felt easy and overflowed without the usual nervousness that can accompany the first sexual encounter that often dampens many couples' dizzying rush into their first taste of lovemaking. They stumbled forward further into the flat. Ray manoeuvred Ella towards the bedroom, covering every part of her exposed flesh with soft, delicate kisses. He removed her shirt, undoing each button until he reached midway, just below her firm breasts. Struggling with yet another ornate circular obstruction that held the fabric together, he gave up the fight and switched tactics. Ray decided at that point that buttons were a hindrance and instead quickly lifted the shirt over Ella's head and removed her lacy lavender bra that was seductively sheer where it needed to be. He cupped each breast in turn and slowly circled his tongue around each areola of her willing mounds. She gasped, inhaling strongly as she felt the desire course through her. She in turn removed Ray's thick, leather belt before lowering his trousers swiftly. They both eagerly fell into a carefully orchestrated dance of pleasure and abandon.

Ray sipped his coffee and crunched into a piece of melon, the juices dripping down his bare chest. Suddenly, the memories of their first time together found themselves at the forefront of his mind. On this Sunday morning, Ray wanted to turn those memories into reality. He bit into the warm croissant and called his girlfriend. Ella responded with a smile. Billy Ocean's *The Colour of Love* blurted out from the radio in the kitchen. By now she knew her boyfriend well enough to know what would happen next.

Six Months Later

Summer was giving up its gifts to autumn's edge; it was the first week in September, and Ella and Ray had settled contentedly into their relationship with many more months and years to look forward to – or so Ray had hoped. It had been the most eventful four months he could recall. The newly in love couple had done everything together. Taken long walks in the Kent countryside (Bedgebury Pinetum_and Scotney Castle were favourites for the easy ambles and rustic scenery), sipped signature coffee in London's latest bijou must-visit spot, talked exhaustively till the early hours, argued to frustration, made love, weighed up the merits of Descartes and Augustine, and discussed half-hatched plans, made love, chewed over cultural and political differences and similarities, made love and put to right the wrongs of the world's great religions. The couple had an immediate connection. Their relationship was growing quickly. It was a relationship that was honest, healthy and each person grew to respect and trust the other. They shared a keen sense of humour, a liking for the arts and a love of food. This allowed room for growth: personal and as a couple. Their relationship was an expression of how two people who would at first glance, not appear to have much in common, found a way to cut through the chaff and connect - intimately and intellectually. Ella's and Ray's backgrounds were different, yet they found common ground in those differences. It was a solid foundation on which their relationship developed. Ray and Ella learnt to appreciate each other's perspectives, each adding to the others bank of experience and knowledge, their interests gelling. Ella's growth mirrored Ray's growth.

As ever, Monday came too quickly, hurriedly pushing aside the gentleness of the weekend. This morning, Ray had to make his way to Homerton, a forgotten part of Hackney in East London where casual, petty crime mixed with serious crime with alarming ease. There had been a spate of fatal stabbings in this part of London over the past few months. Ray was anticipating a grim crime scene and on arriving wasn't to be disappointed. A man and his girlfriend – both, according to police estimates, to be in their early thirties – had obviously got into an intractable domestic argument and the man had lost all sense of reasoning, ran into their tiny kitchen, grabbed a knife and vented his anger on his girlfriend's defenceless, now perforated body.

Sergeant King pulled Ray aside and whispered conspiratorially that this type of crime is all too common but woefully under-reported. "It's normally the black kids knifing other black kids that you typically read and hear about," he said. Sadly, the Man from the Met is probably right, Ray thought to himself.

But he wasn't here to swap gory details with Sgt King. He was working. Ray grabbed his trusted camera and set to work digitally recording every gory detail. Almost every sinew of the victim had been severed by a 10-inch serrated edge. The dark burgundy of decaying blood seemed to ooze slowly out of the woman, meandering in an eerie, steady flow coming to rest sickeningly on the kitchen floor. Ray's photographs would provide vital evidence for medical examiners to determine how the crime was committed. However, in this case there was little doubt. But he had to collect evidence for fingerprint purposes. But Ray was hoping that this time, the brutal and unambiguous nature of the crime meant he did not have to attend court; a junior crime scene officer could do that, he reasoned.

Ray's thoughts turned to Ella. He wanted nothing more than to rush back to her comforting warmth, particularly as she had promised to rustle up a four-bean salad for their evening meal. Ella had been easing Ray gently away from his meat-rich diet that consisted mainly of beef and pork. Being a vegetarian since the age of 14, Ella knew her malabar spinach from her luffa seeds. All Ray had to do was to pick up a bottle of Pinot Noir on the way home.

The murderer, now in handcuffs and in the back of a police van, was Caucasian of presumably Eastern European extraction; Exhibit A: the woman who had been stabbed several times, was blonde, about 5ft 6in, and any distinguishable features were now, well, undistinguishable. Her assailant had made sure of that. Ray photographed the long slice from her left ear to her oesophagus. He also had the unpleasant task of digitally capturing the deep wounds that penetrated her upper left rib, the blade ripping through her breastplate and into her lung. But it was the gorge just above her groin area that nearly made Ray wretch. The fetid stench of violence punctuated the air. It was at moments like this that Ray had to remind himself of all the reasons why he loved his job, but also all the reasons why he wished he would not have to confront scenes like this.

Sergeant King said they'd been in an argument about money: the fact that the assailant didn't have much and expected his girlfriend's legal secretary job to keep him in expensive clothes and equally expensive trainers while he spent his days supposedly looking for work. This led to constant arguments and eventually an unnecessary fatality.

It had been a very difficult day at the office, which was the Metropolitan Police Forensic Science Lab located in a nondescript building in Lambeth, which part of a labyrinth of more nondescript office blocks and a scattering of Peabody Housing Association properties.

But it was where Ray spent a lot of his time on his large computer monitor gathering detailed forensic evidence for the police to use in court cases when necessary. He was good at his job and had a particularly sharp eye for detail, a much-needed skill in this line of work where the conviction or otherwise of a perpetrator can rely on a piece of forensic evidence.

Raymond Gordon started working for the Metropolitan police after having his application for a range of related jobs rejected on no less than 45 occasions. He could not understand why his skills were not immediately apparent to a would-be employer. As far as Ray was concerned, he ticked every box, crossed every T and dotted every i – yet the plumb roles escaped him - repeatedly. But he was surprised, happy and appreciative, when he joined the Met Police. Ray knew, though he was reluctant to admit to the truth, that the piles of rejection letters stored in a large brown manila envelope at home was a reminder that having the necessary qualifications, the right attitude and the correct work ethic was no guarantee of employment. Too often it was the liberal-minded disposition of the recruiter that made the difference to someone meeting the requirements for a particular job vacancy.

It was now 7pm and Ray wouldn't expect to be back in Ella's flat in Brockley till at least 8pm; there were sure to be cancellations on Southern Railway – there always were. On this day, however, he was lucky. No delays, which meant an incident-free journey to the edge of suburban London. Lazily, Ray hung up his well-worn half-length jacket. Unhurriedly, he removed his work clothes. Walked across the wood-stained floorboards with intent, kissed Ella enthusiastically and put the stress of the day behind him with welcome abandon, accompanied by a glass or two of red, and the anticipation of a good meal.

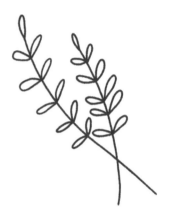

Eight Months Earlier

Raymond Gordon met Ella Somerton-Hughes on an internet dating site. Ray was sceptical about finding a suitable date on these platforms, but Ella proved to be the exception rather than the rule, even though it was Ray's rule, a scepticism that was arrived at from nothing more than a healthy fear of online dating that stood in the way of him accepting the internet as a legitimate option to finding a girlfriend. He thought it was too uncertain, too unregulated and too hit and miss. Ella was raised as a Catholic but had lapsed - rebelliously. But nevertheless, she was still in awe of the indoctrination, the social persuasion and the constraint that had been forced into her very being in her youth. She remembers the recitals of the Catholic church as a form of brainwashing, but the questioning seeds of doubt came at an age when rebellion seemed too dangerous to contemplate.

Ray was a committed not-for-me kind of worshipper, despite his Anglican Christian upbringing and any talk of things Godly would lead to a heated exchange between the couple. He had grown tired of the teachings of the Bible and saw religion as a take-it-or-leave-it interruption to the everyday minutiae of life. Ray was from a strict churchgoing family where the emphasis was on faith, believing in a higher spirit that couldn't be touched but nevertheless held his family in a grip so tight as to be frightening. He had become a half-hearted not-sure believer... sometimes. Atheism was the antithesis of everything Ray's parents believed in. To his mother and father, the Bible was a strict set of instructions on how to live – no deviation. No questions. To Ray, though, it was something that divided nations, pitted brother against sister and neighbour against neighbour. He pointed to almost every military conflict around the world and throughout history as evidence that he was right to hold religion to account for all the ills that are perpetrated by man on his fellow man, and he believed that if his views were right, then his parents' views must be wrong.

But Ray and his brother, Gerald, still had to obey the dictum of constant preaching, the compulsory Sunday school and the learnt deference to authority - and to resist a stubborn urge not to stray too far from the middle ground that his middle-class Jamaican upbringing had confined him to - a conflicted belief system that for him and Gerald was now in tatters. It did, however, and maybe contradictorily, provide Ray with a reason to leave the Church as soon as he was old enough to break free of the suffocating rules and regulations.

That point came when he was no more than 15, despite the best efforts of his mother. At that age, Gerald, who was four years older and considered himself more of a man than a child, acted as a beacon for Ray to follow. So he did. On one hot, sultry July Sunday afternoon in Kingston after spending what seemed like the entire day worshipping a God that Gerald and Ray could/would never meet, the brothers broke the news to their mother and father that they'd "had it with religion and weren't going back to church". That act of single-minded transgression led to a lot of soul-searching in the Gordon household; Mr and Mrs Gordon questioning themselves on where they went wrong and asking for forgiveness – daily – from their omniscient God.

Back A Yard And Back Again

In Jamaica, rum and religion form the perfect, curious contrast of good and bad. The small Caribbean Island of about 2.9 million inhabitants has England to thank for that. The harvesting of sugar that produced rum and the Church of England that brought religion to Jamaica were the two defining signposts of a colonised Jamaica. Black River, a small town in the western edge of the island where crocodile spotting on the eponymous stretch of water is a must, and where the Gordons lived, has 13 churches, emphasising that Jamaica has, per square mile, the highest number of churches in the world, a legacy of when Christianity first came to Jamaica courtesy of Spanish settlers in 1504. But Sundays in Jamaica were for dressing up: the women in their long-sleeved cotton dresses, a fan and a bible, and the men showing off in formal two-piece suits finished with broad, extravagant hats.

The smell of coffee and Ella standing in the morning light jogged Ray's wandering mind back from his past and to present-day reality and to the breakfast Ella had prepared with skill, love and dedication. Ray eyed her up and down with a wide grin on his face. She was the picture of loveliness, the love that he had been hoping to find, a stabilising anchor to his curious, happy-go-lucky mindset.

Ray met Ella after he finished university. He had been in England for 10 years. It was always his family's aim to educate the two brothers in the Motherland, the UK, the coloniser who had charmed and pulled the family into Her promise of a better life, a career and a life of opportunity. The motto of their country, Jamaica, is "Out of Many People, One People". So, Ray reasoned that England would not be anything less than welcoming to this child of the Commonwealth. Ella came into Ray's life after a drunken night out with his university friends who while debating vigorously the pros and cons of settling down or playing the field, managed to convince Ray that the life of a budding player was a waste of time and real men are faithful, loving and generous with their time and themselves. Out of kindness, his university friends could not bring themselves to tell Ray that he was too awkward, too polite, too nice even, to make it as a serious Lothario in the arena of love and seduction. Since arriving from Jamaica, Ray, a fit, good-looking but painfully shy young man, liked the idea of sowing as many wild oats as possible, despite not always being as successful as the impression he liked to give. Ray wanted to broaden his experience beyond what the university campus had to offer and decided that the internet would be his new playground, though he still had reservations about the honesty of some of the dating profiles on many of the sites that he came across.

Ella was not long out of a controlling relationship that had lasted for five years. Five years of what for her was a taste of hell that had eroded her confidence, led her to doubt all and trust few. Her old boyfriend, Steve, wanted marriage and children, and, selfishly, did not consider what Ella's needs and ambitions might be, he did not think that her views were even worthy of consideration. She wanted to explore and grow into the promises of what life had to offer, while he wanted someone to stay at home, cook, clean and have babies. The prospect of a rigid domestic life terrified her and after a while she knew she couldn't stay with Steve any longer and left before it was too late. It was a cold, wet Monday evening when Steve returned home from work when he learnt that his relationship with Ella Somerton-Hughes was over. A three-line hand-written note was all that he received to tell him the news.

"You're suffocating me."

"I need to breathe."

"I'm leaving you."

Ella felt tortured by the blunt way in which she had brought the painful, asphyxiating relationship to a close. It didn't sit easy with her and she decided to tell Nicola, her mother, for fear of being on the receiving end of a lecture about the importance of treating everyone the way in which you wished to be treated. Instead, Ella concocted a story about an old girlfriend of Steve's suddenly popping up from nowhere and he was put in a position where he had to choose, and he chose her. She was never sure that her all-knowing mother bought the story, but she wanted closure on that part of her life so never raised the subject of Steve again, despite the fact that her mother had hopes of advancing her eldest daughter's social status by insisting that she marry Steve as soon as possible. Ella's mother liked the idea of a big wedding where she would be able to show off to her friends and make a statement of how successfully she had brought up her children, especially her eldest daughter, whom she adored and considered nothing was too much for her.

Ella was still getting used to the idea of re-engaging her appetite to the possibility of meeting someone with whom she could at least have a conversation with when Ray turned up. But Ella didn't just drift into Ray's orbit but rather popped into his inbox on one of those many dating sites that allows people to fabricate and obfuscate to their heart's content.

New to this online dating scene, Ray was, despite being engulfed by uncertainty, determined to live up to his carefully constructed Romeo image that he had tried, unconvincingly and unsuccessfully at times, to carve out for himself. Ella, though, was far more experienced than Ray when it came to matters of love, and she was free from her relationship shackles - and loving it. It was not her first foray into the internet dating scene. After her relationship with Steve ended, her first plunge into the world of cyber dating was Frank, a roofer whose outdoorsy lifestyle attracted Ella, who herself was inclined towards sporty endeavours. In Frank, she saw a partner with whom she could share her love of fitness. The fact that he was free and single was a plus too, but soon the physical attraction waned when it became clear that Frank's idea of romance did not go much further than on-demand weekend sex after a too-boozy night out with the boys. It was during one of these many post-pub, drunken attempts at lovemaking when Ella decided that she deserved more than the vacant attention of a boyfriend whose idea of a good night was how little he could remember the next morning.

Then there was Nathaniel, or Nath as he preferred to be called, the lawyer who was so self-absorbed with his own importance and image that the relationship fizzled out before it really took off. The crunch for Ella came when she discovered one Sunday afternoon over wine and canapés in a too expensive eatery for her budget and taste that he spent more on his hair than she did on hers. She was ready to give up internet dating after Daniel, a well-off businessman in his 40s who came with the heavy baggage of an ex-wife who seemed to be calling him endlessly on his mobile phone to remonstrate about one thing or another, but usually about one of the three teenage children they had had in quick succession. After that episode was over, Ella decided she would trust her instincts more, and would therefore cast her net farther and wider and not limit her options. "One last go before a change of dating strategy," she decided, and on a wet February weekend when she was alone but wishing that she wasn't, she grabbed her tablet computer and decided to be spontaneous - even a little daring.

"Fun loving, cheeky, curvy, sensual and down-to-earth 25-year-old looking for... something else."

Ray's response was:

"Hi, I'm Ray."

The brevity of his replay somehow and inexplicably piqued Ella's interest.

"Hidden passions waiting to be discovered," was her response.

Ray: "Hi, I'm six-foot, brown-skinned, handsome, or so I am told, mainly by my mother," was his fumbling, uncertain comeback.

Ella: "I'm a girl who likes discovering new things, new music, new cuisine, I love cooking, and I love hanging out... Message me."

When Ray recomposed his frazzled senses after the openness of this modern-day mating call, he had to admit to himself that he was excited, a little nervous perhaps, but excited nonetheless.

Friends And Acquaintances

P aul Robinson, a philosophy graduate, was Ray's best friend. They had met at university and Ray relied on the erudite and learned Paul to push him through his science degree when all Ray wanted to do was spend as much time as possible in the student union bar getting to know his fellow students, particularly the female undergrads. Paul was a gifted scholar. He cited Walter Rodney and Malcolm X as early influences who framed his views of self-determination for the future of immigrants to this country. Music, though, was Paul's passion, his calling, especially the hidden meaning behind lyrics, which would lead to him spending hours deciphering the metaphors and similes and the assonance that would elicit a particular feeling or meaning behind the seemingly benevolent intention of the best songwriters. Paul saw a hidden meaning in every lyric. Paul Simon, he reasoned, only ever wrote about his personal alienation and religious oppression. Smokey Robinson, in Paul's view, saw the world through the prism of love, cheating and passion while George Michael was the type of songwriter who would use his lyrics to express his angst about just about every close relationship he ever had - male and female - and particularly about his Oedipus complex. For Paul, the message in the song was often more interesting than the song itself. It was this focus that led him to over-analyse and see meaning where there was possibly none. There was a method in Paul's forensic analysis of lyrics and song arrangement: he had ambitions to one day be known as *the* premier lyricist and musical arranger of his generation.

Ray, though, did not have much time for Paul's deep introspection, but he did want to share the internet correspondence from Ella with Paul, who reasoned that Ray was in lust, not love. Nevertheless, Ray convinced himself it was love given that he had never quite managed to nail the lust thing, which all too often turned into a naïve, nervous fumble followed by an embarrassing retreat.

"Whatever..." Ray retorted to Paul's chidings about his friend's lack of appreciation of the finer points of a lyricist's art. However, Ray was smitten by Ella's daring internet posts. For this country boy from Jamaica, Ella represented a scary, bumpy helter-skelter ride that he would hold on to as long as he could, even if he feared that her boldness was a few miles or so outside of his comfort zone. Her Englishness was, as far as Ray was concerned, the best thing of all. She was the living embodiment of all the stories, the literature of the Mother Country, the life of promise, the undiscovered pages yet to be turned. Ella was Ray's Jamaica answering England's calling.

But Ella turned out to be nothing like her flirtatious online dating persona. She was what could be viewed as a typical English girl: funny, clever and with a keen sense of fair play, always rooting for the underdog and recognising injustices whenever and wherever she saw it. As their relationship developed, Ella would always disagree with Ray's "jaundiced" view of England, a perspective, she argued, that was chiselled from 19th-century novels that carried such weight in Ray's island's education system. Ella reasoned that Ray's blinkered love for England and everything English conveniently ignored the racism that ran conveniently unseen, and too often unchallenged, the social and political inequalities, the fact that her privilege and status as a local allowed her to ease her way through life's tricky scrapes; doors opened, and none was ever slammed in her face. But in her would-be boyfriend's eyes, Ella represented the very thing that he was working towards, though at the same time he was beginning to learn about and experience real life on the gilded streets of London, but on a deeper, more pronounced level, one that he had not imagined while in Jamaica harbouring ambitious longings for undiscovered pastures that held the promise of more challenges than what were on offer in Kingston.

In Ray's naïve view of London life, when a young man from the colonies moves to England and achieves even a modicum of success, he had every reason to expect the whole package; the nice car, the expense account, the salary, the material trappings and most of all, the pretty English Rose dangling from his designer suit-wrapped arm. In his eyes, Ella fitted the bill. She was the type of woman who eased her way through life without appearing to have to fight the twin demons of class and race that consigns many people outside of the Oxbridge biosphere to the mediocrity of wanting to but being unable to reach beyond the metaphorical glass ceiling. It was a passage through the twists and turns of society that Ray assumed would be his too. The sobering reality is that society rewards the products of the top schools, the family name is as important as your social contacts and a holiday home in the Dordogne or Chianti is in the right circles seen as the true mark of success. With an education the product of The Girls' Day School Trust and solidly middle-class upbringing, Ella had very little to worry about, though socially conscious parents had given her a grounded, world view. She had graduated from the London School of Economics and headed for the financial hub of Canary Wharf and a job as an account manager for a global digital company. She loved her job, which involved maintaining relationships with existing customers and to seek out new markets and opportunities for her clients.

Ella was fastidious in her work and did not tolerate nonsense away from the office; she would rail against anything that she perceived as being unfair – even if it wasn't. At nearly six-feet tall in her high heels, Ella was not someone you missed. Her naturally thick, dark hair, these days Henna-tinted, tumbled in lustrous tendrils on night's out, but was more often worn up to reveal her high cheekbones, a feature inherited from her father, Stephen, and her mother's broad shoulders that would too often invite guesses from strangers that she was an elite-class swimmer or rower, or more often than she appreciated, would attract the gaze of men. A regular fitness routine that involved mainly running, maintained her impressive physical presence.

For Ella, though, Ray was simply a sweet, nerdy, interesting if a little lost, guy. His heritage and culture did not present a barrier to her, though she feared it might present a barrier to others and challenge the carefully constructed concept of multiculturalism that London welcomed and was famous for. It was when she met Ray and the attraction cemented itself in her psyche that she really understood Martin Luther King's "I have a Dream" speech. It really was about the content of Ray's easy-going, effervescent character that she found to be more appealing than the colour of his skin, and after a controlling, potential psychopath, a narcissist and a sex-obsessed loser, Ella was relieved that Ray offered her intellectual stimulation, light-hearted fun, a modicum promise of safety, someone who she could trust and who didn't arrive carrying a skip-full of issues and who would love her for who she was.

When Ella and Ray were together, she would stop, look, even stare at Ray, and traced the outline of his features with her mind, recalling how smooth and reassuring his face felt, her thoughts running over every familiar etched contour and fold. It was a contrast to his hard-to-fathom mind that would without instigation or provocation slip ever so easily into a contented state of devil-may-care. Ray had an enviable ability to put troubles behind him. It was a feature that Ella wished that she could muster up when needed. But annoyingly, she couldn't. In Ella's mind, you are either born with the disposition of a Zen god or not. And Pasithea she was not. She would worry about anything and everything - often unnecessarily and to her detriment. Ray, though, at any time and in any situation, appeared not to be disconcerted by anything.

When Ray is in these self-reflective moods, he often looks at Ella and draws her, not with a pen or a brush the way an artist would sketch the outline of a muse in readiness for the finishing touches and strokes that would transform an idea to a fully fledged painting, but with a gesture, a smile, a look or a gaze. These moments often left Ella feeling exposed, but she welcomed this non-sexualised attention. At times, such attention is either unwanted or not suited to the moment. But theirs was an exchange of non-verbal communication, mutual respect and appreciation. At moments like these, Ella would stir from these suspended seconds of near somnambulism to wrap herself cosily into Ray's embrace.

Great Expectations

Ray knew from an early age that he was clever. His father and mother raised Ray and his brother with the expectation that they would do well in life. Mr and Mrs Gordon understood the benefits of a good education and told their boys that nothing was unattainable, and nothing was out of reach for them. All it took was commitment, focus and determination. Coming to a cosmopolitan city like London did not change Ray's outlook and he quickly rejected the too many negative influences open to a young black man, such as gangs, becoming involved negatively with the police and dropping out of mainstream society. He simply couldn't understand the nihilistic mentality of the many British-born black boys that he encountered in the UK. Coming from Jamaica, the Jamaica that he was familiar with, it was not the type of behaviour that he recognised or aspired to.

Ray's father, Cecil, and his mother, Janice, had life planned out for their boys. Deviation from the script was just not part of the deal, not an option. They would get a good education, go to university and settle into brilliant careers – and marry a "nice brown-skin girl". In some ways that was Ray's undoing in his parents' eyes: he didn't find his "nice brown-skin girl", but a woman of much fairer complexion.

However, both boys, mostly, kept their part of the bargain and both did well educationally and materially. All their parents had to do was be there for them and encourage them, which they were and did unconditionally. Cecil and Janice came to England at a time when being professionals in Jamaica wasn't enough to satisfy their ambition. In Jamaica it was normal to see policemen, educators, politicians, doctors, businesspeople.... Every public figure, every icon, every TV personality or role model was black. So normal, in fact, to Ray, a society made up of a kaleidoscope of people didn't register as anything unusual. In England at a time when Cecil and Janice migrated to England, a black face in a position of authority in the UK was rare. It was a time that Ray's parents found difficult.

Both were maths teachers in Kingston, Jamaica's bustling, edgy capital that stretched out along the south-eastern coast of the island with the Blue Mountains as its backdrop. It is from these towering peaks that the famous Blue Mountain Coffee is grown and shipped around the world. But things were very different in England. Rather than teaching, Cecil could only find work driving buses and Janice had to settle, begrudgingly, for work as a hospital auxiliary nurse. Their qualifications and experience were not recognised in the United Kingdom. Resigned to the new rules imposed by their adopted country, they had the choice of starting over again, or falling in line with expectations. They turned their focus on their boys. Their own personal ambition and a vision of achieving something in the country they regarded as the place to be after having been enamoured with all things Royal and British, was put to one side. Their efforts were transferred to Gerald and Ray. Entranced by the lure of England, they saw their nirvana for them and their two boys in London. Lofty dreams of a better life drove them to England's cold climate, leaving behind the effervescent colour, the cool breeze, the fragrant mango trees, the ubiquitous Blue Mahoe tree, and the sunshine of the Caribbean.

Cecil and Janice instilled in their two boys a self-confidence that seems to be lacking in people of Caribbean parentage who were born in the UK. After graduating from university with a first in Biological Science, Ray pursued a career in forensic photography, a path he decided would be his route to success – a geek with an edge he reasoned. The career allowed for academia and creativity in tandem and would channel Ray's talents through the lens of a camera. He could see nothing before him but unbridled success and with success comes reward. Ray expected the rapid promotion that never came and would remain as elusive as trying to wrestle down the wind with his bare hands.

But his imagined success was the unsullied ambition of a young man who believed that the concept of hard work and talent would be enough to take him to the top of his chosen profession. It proved to be naïve. He would continually stub his toe on life's invisible rocks. Ray was fighting against a noxious mix of privilege and slavery that gave birth to a nascent class system that built its foundations and pillars of elitism, on sugar, on coco, and on tobacco. The boy from the Caribbean was blithely expecting to progress through a system that did not allow for outliers – whether from the Caribbean or the mining towns of South Yorkshire. It would be many years and many disappointments before Ray understood the workings of the secretive narrow corridors of the British class system that, despite appearances to the contrary, subtly and carefully only allowed the privileged elite to progress to the seats of power.

Promises Of Spring

Two months after their cyber introduction, and digital flirtations via a computer screen, Ella and Ray decided to throw off the anonymous cloak of the internet chat rooms and meet in person. That event took place on a warm but hazy spring morning. They decided to browse around an old bookshop in Greenwich, a quaint, once neglected but now expensive part of south London that was regarded as the full stop to this part of the capital. But it is revered and celebrated with an in-the-know nudge and wink by most South Londoners.

Appreciation came, too, from the thousands of tourists who responded to the call of the celebrated and historic sailing ship that was the fastest clipper of its time, the Cutty Sark, the small but perfectly maintained Greenwich Park, which was once the playground of Henry VIII, and the Meridian Line that attracts tourists from far and wide. The area also attracts new money, people who could no longer afford to buy in Islington, Clapham and Camden because of spiralling house prices in those areas, and who wanted to keep their postcode cool and still enjoy the hustle and bustle of communal wanderings for bric-a-brac and the occasional pause for a cappuccino or iced latte. Ella's flat was a short train ride from Greenwich's buzzing centre, therefore making it close enough to the market and to the gym to which she paid her expensive monthly membership fee, now occupying a spot on the newly built complex that was once the site of the local hospital.

Ella wanted to visit Hardy's in Greenwich Church Street to satisfy her craving for sweets from the 70s. Ray had been after a copy of The War Broadcasts of George Orwell by W J West for a long time and was told by a bookish university friend that Taylor's Bookshop on the north side of the one-way system in Greenwich is the only place likely to have it. Ray and Ella decided to meet up in the local coffee shop after the bookshop and the sweetshop. Ray's friend proved the font of knowledge. Taylor's Bookshop did, indeed, have a dusty copy of the book. As Ray reached for the long-neglected book, which had obviously been lying unloved and unwanted on the bookshelf for so many years it was clear the owner had forgotten it was there, a walnut-brown, elegant hand also reached out from apparently nowhere targeting the same book. Ray was gripped by a feeling of dread. Was he going to play Sir Galahad and allow the hand to bag his long-searched-for prize? Was he about to lose his book?

No. He grabbed and the hand grabbed, both gripping tightly, neither daring to let go. Ray glared deep into the woman's eyes, giving her his best "I'm-being-serious" look. She returned a warm, confident smile. The antagonist resisted Ray's every tug; she countered every pull with her small but vice-like grip while boring right through Ray with her best "this-belongs-to-me" stare. She was about five feet five in height, but she appeared like a giant as she challenged and dared Ray to liberate the book from his grasp and release it into her possession. Under normal circumstances he would have given way, but this time he was determined not to play the good guy. He wanted the book.

"Do you like Orwell," Ray asked, immediately saying to himself that that was the silliest question he had ever posed – anywhere or to anyone. "If I didn't like the man's work, I wouldn't be prepared to cut up rough with you for one of his books, would I now?" was Ms Mahogany-Brown's sharp riposte. Ray was taken aback, unable to respond, although he wanted to put her in her place with a carefully crafted verbal riposte, snatch the book from this angelic brute and get the hell out of the shop. The clever volleyed response from Ray never materialised.

"It's obvious we both want the same book and as there is only one copy. I'll make a deal with you," she said.

"Deal? Not likely," Ray said while all the time refusing to let go of Orwell's war recollections. Ray stared, waiting for another salvo. It came.

"Look," she said. "I want this book. I'm writing a paper on the politics of language for my Master's degree and I need to study Orwell to gauge the nationalistic feeling of the day and who better to capture the nation's linguistic idiosyncrasies and thoughts than George Orwell. Once I finish with it, I'll let you have it - if you share the cost with me. That will ensure that I keep my part of the bargain... I will only need it for about three weeks."

Shocked by the audacity and the inventiveness of the proposal, the bare-faced cheek and wit of it, and annoyed because he had allowed himself to be manipulated by this woman, Ray mumbled rather pathetically, "sure, why not." The woman smiled, demanded, and received £8 from Ray to meet the cost of his share of the cover price, then introduced herself as Michelle Stewart. They exchanged names and addresses and Michelle waltzed out of the shop. "Stupid!" Ray remonstrated with himself, wondering if he would ever see the book again. What hadn't occurred to Ray was that seeing the book again would involve seeing her again. He was still reeling from the exchange and didn't particularly want to have to do that, yet he could not suppress the idea of once more meeting Michelle.

Standing by the shop's entrance was Ella, who had witnessed this comical exchange. As Michelle sauntered through the exit, Ella who had by this time grown tired of waiting for Ray to arrive at the coffee shop, gave her a piercing, quizzing look. She had seen her before but could not remember where or when.

Exactly three weeks had gone by, and Ray had given up all hope of ever seeing Orwell's The War Broadcasts again and had kissed his eight quid goodbye. "That eight pounds could have been used to buy a bottle or two of beer. Shit!" Ray exclaimed.

It was 9am, and Ray was in his flat doing nothing much, which for a young man who seemed not to have a care in the world, was the best thing to do on a Sunday morning. Especially this Sunday morning when the early hours ushered in a calm that allowed for pensive reflection. Ray decided to go through the papers, a weekly ritual that he enjoyed because it meant that he could stall the start of any chores a little longer. The sports section of the Observer was the best while the arts section of The Sunday Times always had something to stir his interest; for news he once again turned to the Observer and the frilly silly lascivious title-tattle of the Mail on Sunday was left to last once the serious stuff was out the way.

It was the last week in May and the warm morning light streaming through Ray's lounge window hinted at the promise of a brilliant summer to come. It was the type of morning that would inspire walks in the park and lazy afternoons before having to confront the routine of Monday morning and the necessity of the office or another messy police incident. He was flicking through the news sections of the quality newspapers when his morning was interrupted by the sound of his doorbell: a sound that he wasn't expecting. He certainly wasn't anticipating a visitor.

"Hi, I bet you didn't expect me to return the book," Michelle said standing on Ray's budget door mat and looking not like how he remembered her. With a large black beret that sat unconvincingly on her head, her long locks sneaking out from the corners of the soft hat, the dappled morning light made her honey-brown skin somehow less striking and more ordinary than Ray's memory had created. However, he could not deny her captivating allure. Michelle had caught Ray off-guard.

"Frankly, no," he said. "But you didn't have to bring it round. The postal service still works, you know, it's not great but it still works."

"I was curious," Michelle said, still holding the book and squeezing her way past Ray and into his two-bedroom first-floor flat on the borders of Blackheath and Lewisham. He got lucky when he bought this flat. It was just after the property collapse of the mid-Nineties and Ray had a bit of cash stashed away from some shrewd buying and selling of shares courtesy of a friend that he knew who worked in the City. The friend helped him to navigate the buying and selling of other peoples' money. Corporate gambling, he called it. Ray thought it was a great way of accumulating a quick stash of cash, although he also realised it was a great way to lose a lot of money too – that's why he got out when the going was good. One company in his portfolio had gone belly up after a period of over-expansion. It was enough to give Ray cold feet. A few bloody noses aside, what made playing the financial markets such fun was the fact that a lot of his friends thought that he was weird and not "acting black enough". "We as black people don't do dem tings," they would remonstrate. Maybe! Ray thought at that moment that he should change the company he keeps. But while his friends splashed out every week on the National Lottery for no return for their devotion to the little come-hither numbers and slaved and saved long and hard to buy the latest German performance car, Ray kept his eyes on the FTSE-100 and was steadily building up a profitable portfolio that could, given careful planning, some luck and a good broker, net tens of thousands in one hit. And a zone 1-4 Oyster travel card was all the transport he needed.

The two-bed converted flat in a large Victorian house with all its original features was the successful result of such flurries and cost just over five hundred thousand pounds, expensive at the time, but it came with the right post code, so Ray jumped feet first into the property market. A large deposit kept the mortgage low enough for Ray to give the impression that he had more money than he actually did. He learnt soon after arriving in the UK that giving the right impression is everything in a society that builds its reputation on materialism and having the right accoutrements to make the intended statement.

Back on the steps of said flat, Michelle stood. "Curious?" Ray said to Michelle, looking at her and trying to remember if he had invited her in, or if he should be completely unreasonable and send her packing.

"Yeah," she said. "I wanted to see what type of man would agree to my going Dutch over a book and had not given it to me as an act of outright and unconditional chivalry."

This time, Ray was ready. "First, my acquiring the book is worth more to me than you are, and second, you've got a bloody cheek coming around here uninvited telling me that I should have given you the book in the first place. And it's so early in the morning... don't you sleep? And what made you think I would be in.... What if I had company...".?

"Now, now," Michelle said, "and I had you down as an OK kind of guy, besides I live in the area. Is that coffee I smell? Java? No, it's more subtle... a blend of some sort. South American? I have a keen sense of smell, you know."

She was by now already in Ray's flat and heading for the kitchen wriggling her way out of her waist-length black denim jacket. Her too-big hat was by now off. For his part, Ray wondered if he should thank her for the book and point her in the direction of the bus stop. Instead, he said. "Yes, it is, and no, it's not a blend, but it is South American, Colombian to be precise. Would you like some?"

Michelle took her coffee black arguing that sugar and milk spoils the taste and ruins the flavour. She declined Ray's offer of croissants and fried plantain on account of her having already eaten breakfast and proceeded to sip rather than guzzle his finest South American brew.

"Aren't you being a bit brave coming here," Ray asked. "I could be the misogynist from hell or worse." He waited for a smart response.

"I'm a good judge of character and when I met you in the bookshop in Greenwich, I knew you were harmless. If I had any doubts you would not have seen me or the book again," Michelle came back.

"So why are you here, apart from keeping up your end of the deal. Is this some sort of come-on?"

"Don't flatter yourself Raymond," she spat back.

"It's Ray, actually. Everyone calls me Ray."

"As I said Raymond, don't flatter yourself. You're cute if the light catches you the right way but I'm not looking for someone to keep me warm at night. Besides, what I look for in male company has more to do with what's in his head than what's in his trousers."

Ray decided that it was not the time, and he was not in the mood to take her on. It was Sunday morning after all and no time for fighting with an almost stranger. Besides, Ella is known to drop by unannounced; and Ray did not want to have to explain why a strange woman was in his flat so early on a Sunday morning. No amount of explanation would appease Ray's English Rose.

"Was the book useful," Ray asked with all-too obvious irritation and timbre to his voice that suggested he was struggling to make conversation. Her poise and confidence had again caught him off guard and unsettled him, and the idea that she may have thought that he was trying to get inside her pants embarrassed him, though he did, in his mind, have an eye for the ladies – and a self-applied reputation to cultivate. Ray was handsome in a rugged sort of way. His high cheekbones and ripped body were immediate eye candy, but Ray realised early on in his journey around London's hot spots that confidence and bravado counted more than good looks when winning over women. Michelle was the kind of woman that would present a challenge to his sense of masculinity.

On this occasion, though, Ray knew that he should have asked Michelle to leave, but for some unfathomable reason he wanted to ask her if he could see her again but decided that that would be too presumptuous, too stupid and it would invite opprobrium. And he wasn't single.

Ray battled with his common sense and his libido, reaching a point where he would have said anything but knew that whatever came out of his mouth would have sounded as if the words were coming from a nerdy schoolboy on his first date with no idea how to speak to the opposite sex. He looked deep into Michelle's eyes, the eyes that had put a spell on him three weeks earlier. She looked straight back and smiled sweetly. Silence was, indeed, the most eloquent option Ray had at his disposal at that time.

"Thanks for the coffee," Michelle said, grabbed her beret and jacket and headed for the door. Ray followed her half out of politeness and half because he could not help it. This action was, of course, against his better judgement. He had not invited the feeling that this woman had again got the better of him, but he couldn't contain it.

"Goodbye Raymond," she said and was out the door.

"Ray", he called out feebly. "It's Ray," followed by the weedier utterance, "can I call you?" Even if the fleet-footed woman had heard his limp request, she would have ignored it. Ray felt strange. He was touched by this confident, intriguing woman?

Michelle's sassiness unnerved, even alarmed, a lot of men, men who mistook her ease and confidence for arrogance. While she was extremely particular about her choices in love, it was her ambition to succeed as a specialist in language that fuelled her drive, and it was that determination that gave her most pleasure in life. She didn't have a compelling reason to indulge the time-consuming distractions of the male kind.

"Where did she come from?" Ray wondered. He smiled and recoiled back into his flat and returned to the Sunday papers.

After Michelle left, Ray was flushed with excitement and called Paul. "Hey, guess what? You know that girl with the neat locks that bagged my book in Greenwich, she called round,"

Paul's reply was muted to the point of boredom.

"Who called round," came the perplexed reply. "And why are you phoning me so early anyway? What girl? What's happened to your girl?"

"It's not that early, in fact it's 11.30 in the morning and besides, you are too old to be raving until daylight, a time when most people are waking up."

"No. You're too old, or at least you act like you're old, and it sounds as if you've been had," growled Paul clearly not in the mood to hear Ray's early morning ramblings of, in Paul's mind, a distant and fleeting meeting with a random woman Ray had recently told him about. Paul was more interested in catching up on his sleep after a night of clubbing that had continued into the early hours.

Reading Between The Lines

Although Ray met Paul at university and although their career choices had taken them down very different roads, the two men remained good friends. Paul was one of those itinerant jobbing musicians whose true passion was writing songs, which explains why he's always out till the early hours watching the next big thing on the music scene in the hope of penning a hit for them. Paul played piano and bass guitar as well as most and could even make people sit up and take notice on the saxophone. His musical appreciation was eclectic, enjoying the likes of Jimi Hendrix to Travis. His was the bass licks you often heard on TV commercials and is the bass heard on any number of top 10 hits. But Paul did not mind the anonymity of the session player, his real interest was writing lyrics and song arrangements – the more political, the better. Paul would try to educate his friend into the teachings of Marcus Garvey and W.E.B Du Bois. Ray, though, wasn't interested, considering his friend too politically biased for his own good, often mocking his choice of reading material, which would guarantee to give rise to Paul's irritation and would inevitably lead to him accusing Ray of being a Philistine. Ray, though, preferred the more easy-going aspects of being a young man living in London. He liked the café culture, the range of theatre offerings and the diversity that cannot be accessed in many of the world's capital cities. It was a world away from what he had been used to in Kingston, his only recollection of a city with the same buzz and urgency as London was New York, which he had the good fortune to visit on more than one occasion given its relatively short four-hour flight from Kingston.

"Ray? What is it with you and this girl? Leave it alone, man... never known you like this over some skirt... and what about Ella? Aren't you two supposed to be tight and shit? This girl sounds way out of your league anyway. Ray, I think you should stay in your lane instead of trying to reach further than your arms are able to stretch. From what you've told me about this woman, she'll eat you up and spit you out in a nano-second.

"No, no, listen Paul, me and Ella are cool, it's just that Michelle... well, she's intriguing, neat, a looker, she fascinates me... I don't know why, but she just does. And, yes, I know I've just clapped eyes on her."

"Yeah! It sounds like you and your lady are cool. Jus' wait till she finds out you're giving time to another woman," said Paul. "Look, man, call me later, when I've had my full eight hours kip."

Paul hung up before Ray could elicit from his friend complicit approval of any would-be philandering.

Paul Robinson was an independent free spirit. His time at university was no more than a conduit to further developing a questioning mind. When he wasn't playing or writing music, he was reading. Dystopian novels such as Aldous Huxley's Brave New World, and Fahrenheit 451 by Ray Bradbury, thrillers from Stephen King and John Grisham, and anything by Charles Dickens were staples, but he also danced to the lyricism of Zora Neale Hurston and Langston Hughes. He ate up Aristotle, Zola and Jean-Paul Sartre and hungrily consumed anything around philosophy, phenomenology, history, and literature to a point where he became an expert - well in his mind anyway. But it wasn't enough. He wanted to be part of every conversation, to fit in, to always have a valid contribution to any conversation.

Paul's reading list had enabled for a rounded education that meant he could challenge the most enthusiastically argued point with a convincing rebuttal. Slavery naysayers were quickly and mercilessly put down. Conspiracy theorists were given short shrift. Those on the right of the political divide were left doubting their conviction after daring to challenge Paul's left-leaning politics. But somewhere along the way that thirst for knowledge turned into a hardened militancy, but Paul preferred to present an affable front, a position that he realised enabled him to establish and nurture contacts in the music industry that furnished a comfortable standard of living and a useful contact book. This course of action was preferable to railing against the system. As a black man he knew the importance of playing his cards right, presenting an approachable side to satisfy booking agents. It was a subtle, manipulative tactic that he had learnt, but this was the price he had to pay for the below-the-surface racism that permeates the seemingly egalitarian melting pot of London. Paul did not like having to fall in line and would fight against what he saw as the injustices that lurked around every corner.

"Your name please," called the anonymous looking man in an ill-fitting grey suit holding a clip-board full of names. Paul responded. Unzipped his bass guitar from its protective case. The brief was simple: play a two-minute piece that had to be note perfect. The reward was a television advert that would keep Paul's bank balance topped up for the foreseeable future. "Thank you, Mr Robinson. The agency will get back to you." The short sentence was familiar. It was full of promise and hope, but nothing to show at the end. Paul had heard these words enough times to know that it was shorthand for "The agency won't get back to you".

Paul's affable demeanour was disappearing fast. "I am fed up with this. Fed up! Fuck! Another audition, another rejection. I am losing out on another commission because of... what, I don't know. I can't understand what these recruitment agencies are looking for, certainly not someone who is actually any good. They are all full of it... all of them, and I know that there wasn't another musician there today who was note perfect - as I was. I am sick of this rejection crap." On the way out from the audition, Paul kicked the exit door as hard as he could, the flimsy frame of the wooden door shook in defiance of Paul's thrusting boot, his anger and frustration spilling over for all to see, his anxiety growing as his mind swirled while searching for answers. He questioned the motives of the recruitment agency, and his anger grew further and his confusion increased. "I'm suspicious of those so-called talent spotters in this industry. They wouldn't know a bass clef from a slap around the face. Shit! What am I going to do now? There's got to be more to this than waiting on the generosity of some tone-deaf bastard to hand out morsels to working players like me. Fuck! Fuck...!" he exclaimed, the dark clouds of uncertainty gathering. It had become apparent to Paul that despite his erudition, his university degree, his musical skill, his experience, and his extensive reading list, he was not being judged on his ability as a musician.

Almost a week had gone by since that Sunday morning when Michelle bid Ray farewell outside his flat and strolled slowly down his tree-lined road till the left turn to the station took her out of Ray's sight. And she had not called. Ray began to wonder if she had crumpled up the piece of paper on which he had carefully written his mobile number and thrown it in the gutter.

"Paul, she hasn't called." Paul had met Ray in the West End. Paul was checking out the latest garage releases from Purple Disco Machine, Deborah de Luca and Charlotte de Witte and some Indy stuff Ray didn't much care for. "And I thought you'd ask about that advert gig I auditioned for last week.

"Yeah, I meant to. How did it go?"

"Not great," Paul responded. "I didn't get it. Yet another kick in the teeth. The best paid jobs somehow are always just out of my reach. I wonder why? It's just as well that I am not short of work. Bass for hire, that's me."

"You spend all your money on rubbish records, anyway," Ray teased, trying to ease the tension on Paul's face. "You should check out some D'Angelo and Jill Scott... real riddim and blooze," Ray emphasised. "Nah mate, D'Angelo's cool but it's all in the mix these days, you don't have black music or white music anymore, it's just music, you just don't get it... r'n'b, reggae, pop, it's all the same, the lines of popular music are blurred... get with the programme Ray, man. The world is changing, and you're being left behind.... Who hasn't called?"

"Michelle," Ray responded. "She said she'd call, and she hasn't. I find that my mind is distracted towards her when I'm pouring over some grisly image on the computer screen at work. It's been so long since I saw you dating anyone that you probably don't remember what it's like to feel that buzz, do you?" Ray teased.

"What's with this woman, man?" asked Paul.

"She's a fine-looking woman," Ray said in defence of Michelle. On cue, Paul said: "You hardly know her. She might turn out to be very different from how you imagine her to be. You never really know someone, even if you are eager to get to know them. Women are funny creatures. When you think you know them, they turn against you and become something else completely. Or in some cases, someone else. Be careful, Ray, you might get burned. When am I gonna meet Mystery Lady, anyway?"

Before Ray could answer, Paul said, "Listen to this groove, man. It's kicking... and the lyrics are on point...." Paul had clearly lost interest in Ray's imaginary love life with Mystery Lady and had turned his attention to the next track in his musical wonderland.

Paul would indeed meet Michelle, but not in a conventional way. Michelle possessed the type of physical beauty that turned the head of most. Attracting the attention of men was not a problem for Michelle. Her long, natural locks framed her strong, high cheekbones and her exquisite fashion sense was so finely tuned that she had a knack of picking just the right cut and style to compliment her shapely body. She worked as a specialist insurance broker for entertainers, providing cover for those the ordinary broker would be too nervous and risk-averse to take on. As a musician whose work took him far and wide to satisfy a variety of clients, Paul fell into this category. But their meeting was not pre-arranged, nor in person, but through the daily passage of Michelle's work when she had to create a bespoke policy for a "Paul Robinson", who was travelling to Russia for an advertising shoot, supplying the music in conjunction with a renowned balalaika player, and needed his expensive bass covered for loss and damage. The name "Paul Robinson" did not yet mean anything to Michelle. He was just another entertainer to be serviced with the right insurance cover.

Paul liked visiting Russia, it was not his first time in its capital city, Moscow, and its hidden haunts was where someone like Paul could let down his carefully constructed guard in the anonymity of the invitation-only underground clubs where discretion is guaranteed. Paul's Moscow wasn't the image that everyone in the West had bought into. The area around Bolotny Island drew the trendy, arty Muscovites as well as the curious visitor looking for the unusual, the risky, the type of entertainment that you only heard about if you knew the right people. And in Moscow, Paul knew who to call. Bolotny Island is one of Moscow's most creative areas, home to the city's progressive and exclusive nightclubs, as well as galleries, bars, and trendy coffee shops. The Red October Factory was where you could hang out without attracting the watching eyes and the inevitable censorship of those who would enforce a particular way of life in Moscow. It was a type of hiding place where anxiety was removed and a lifestyle that Paul enjoyed in London was there for him to lose himself in without fear or favour. To Paul, this was a side of Moscow that he loved to embrace, a side that is deliberately hidden from the popular preconceived perception of most people. In Moscow, Paul could be whoever he wanted to be, he was not confined by the constraints of convention and expectation, here he was able to express himself openly. Paul did not consider himself as promiscuous but preferred the label of freedom: neither straight nor gay, not attached, but free to make decisions based on how he felt at a given time. There were no consequences, and Moscow accommodated the level of anonymity that was not always readily available in London where his reputation as a skilled musician preceded him. England's capital had a deserved reputation of being open and free. But unlike Moscow, London was a city where you could not hide, even if you wanted to.

Paul returned to Heathrow five days later. He was met at the airport by Ray and Ella because Ella was the only one of the three who owned a car, furthermore, a car large enough to accommodate three adults and a large, delicate bass guitar.

"Akwaaba," was the short but appreciative greeting from Paul, a gentle and polite peck on the cheek was extended to Ella. The deliberate but heartfelt slip into the traditional Ghanaian greeting was lost on Ella - and Paul.

"You'd better thank Ella, she's the one who agreed to schlep all the way to Heathrow to pick you up. Do you have any idea how bad London traffic is on a Sunday morning," Ray asked? The two friends chatted away animatedly, mostly Ray trying to extract from Paul every drop of tittle-tattle and nocturnal carry-on about the Moscow trip, and the banter and exaggerated tales of his trip only paused when Paul asked Ella if he could borrow her phone to call his mother. "She always gets worried when I'm away on business. I don't know why she does, I'm a grown man who can look after himself. But I suppose mothers will be mothers, and if I don't call her the minute I'm back in ole' Blighty, she panics; thinks I have been kidnapped by men in long black coats who wear dark glasses at night and hide behind newspapers," Paul said with a laugh. "My phone ran out of juice on the last day in Moscow and I couldn't find my charger." A dead phone was reasonable grounds for asking to borrow Ella's.

For Ella's part, lending Paul her phone to call his mother did not seem unusual given the closeness of her boyfriend and his friend. There was no reason to question or deny his request. Paul and Ray were always swapping things, lending this and borrowing that – nothing was off limits between the two men. It could be money; it could be clothes. Both men would think nothing of giving their time to each other, often to the complete disregard of the needs of anyone else, whether it was a close relative, a close friend; or even Ella.

As they drove through London, Ella drank in the easiness of the capital city, the traffic criss-crossing its way through the twists and turns of the road system, a template of rat-runs and short cuts that had become part of this city's DNA, a learnt navigational instinct as much as a physical map that had become fossilised in the minds of all who lived, loved and lost in the huge expanse of life that is London. Ella also allowed her mind to drift to a time earlier in the year, on another occasion when she was driving through London. The journey reminded her of the crisp spring day when she met Paul for the first time and how strange he seemed when Ray introduced her to his best friend. She thought he was an interesting addition to her boyfriend's cohorts of mismatched, even oddball acquaintances, but nothing more. When Ray told her that Paul was a musician, she was not surprised: it fitted the controlled edginess of Paul. "Pleased to meet you," she offered. "Likewise," came the warm, if muted response.

Ella was acutely aware that not all of Ray's friends might be as egalitarian as her boyfriend, despite the city's well-known reputation for cultural diversity and the mingling and mixing cheek by jowl of different people in a gloriously harmonious way that, as far as Ella was concerned, benefits everyone. She had a habit, rather a want, to see the good in everyone. She had read about the no-go areas of London, the supposed enclaves of Irish settlers, Jamaicans, Nigerians, East End hardened "bovver" boys, young men who would actively go looking for trouble after a few too many pints, the Asians, the Eastern Europeans, the Arabs.... Despite London's reputation for mixing cultures, these cultures didn't always mix. Tension could fester. If you wandered into the wrong postcode, wore the wrong type of trainer, or the wrong hoodie, it could spell trouble. London was like a throw and a catch: two different sides - the dangerous, dark side and the all-embracing, inclusive, welcoming side. You just had to know how to tip-toe skilfully around both personalities of the capital to move through the various areas of London without being noticed or singled out. Londoners knew instinctively how to move in and out of the nooks and crannies of the city without arousing unwanted attention. Ella knew the heartbeat of the city having grown up on its outskirts and would, with her little sister, Rebecca, take the train to Oxford Street and Regent's Street to spend their saved-up pocket money on the latest fashions. Topshop on the corner of Oxford and Regent's Streets was always a favourite go-to destination. Clubbing and partying in the east, the north and the south of the capital did not present any barriers for the two adventurous young women. It was a lifestyle that they had enjoyed since they were in their late teens and early twenties and they were, therefore, comfortable with the many faces of London.

Ella instinctively drove straight to Ray's flat, pulling up outside on the correct assumption that a late lunch, beer and more boys' banter would be in order, and so it proved. As the two men slinked away to get on with their boys' stuff, Ella excused herself and retreated to Ray's bedroom and curled up with a book and nestled in among the soft down pillows, pillows that reminded her of pink fluffy petals that fall from trees in the bright spring sunshine. It was a time of year that she looked forward to because it signalled a sense of comfort, of longer days, froth-covered cappuccinos, the emergence of warm nights and soft slippers and new beginnings.

But as she slipped into her dream-like space, she could still hear the uninhibited and uproarious laughter coming from the nearby front room, but she was oblivious to its detail, but nevertheless she smiled to herself happy in the knowledge that Ray was happy. She hugged the soft pillows to her breast. She too felt happy.

When Ella met Ray, she was only too aware that too many men on the first date focus too eagerly on the end goal, press go, and ignore everything in between. Ella's mother always told her that men in general fail to understand that the way to true fulfilment and satisfaction in life is via the mind, not elsewhere on the anatomy, though despite her mother's warnings, Ella often wondered what was so wrong with short-circuiting the maze-like games men and women play if all you wanted was the appetising dessert. However, in the presence of her mother she would keep these thoughts strictly to herself. As Ella absorbed the words on the page of her book, her mind drifted to her mother's oft-repeated mantra on how to skip around the bumpy road of relationships, which repeated in her subconscious as she read. "When we meet like-minded people the pieces of the jigsaw fall into place, only then do we begin to discard the disjointed, ill-fitting elements that create those obstinate obstacles to true love…"

Ella had a habit of recalling her mother's musings at odd times. She would marvel at how much her over-cautious, protective proverbs such as "protecting yourself is your only self-defence," or "Sometimes, staying away from people is the only protection that you have," would stick. But Ella's favourite mother-saying was "Safety is an illusion". Too often, she found that her mother's wagging finger would barge uninvited into her conscious mind.

Summer Days

It was another typical Thursday evening; the summer days were long, and the evenings were warm. Annoyingly for Ella, Ray had fallen into a pattern of working late on Thursdays. The workload always seemed to increase the closer to the weekend the week drew. This Thursday evening was no different from those of the past few months: a cycle of work piling up, a late, exhausting finish and home. Ray was troubled by the frequency of gang-related stabbings that were happening: jobs that he had to photograph. At that moment he was thankful he did not have to engage with the families of the latest young life to be lost to the senseless violence that was washing over the capital like a stench.

Thursdays was when Ella chose to use the time when Ray was at work to go to the gym. This evening she wanted to work on her glutes and her external obliques. "Some deadlifts and some glute bridge to leg raises," Ella reasoned. About six months earlier she had engaged the services of a personal trainer. She had recently joined the gym with the aim of strengthening her core with the aim ultimately of taking part in the London Marathon. She wanted to make a difference and raising money for charity with her efforts over the gruelling 26 miles and 385 yards appealed to her. She wasn't overly enthusiastic about training with weights, not wanting to put on too much bulk, but she thought that she would soon reach a stage of practise and knowledge where she could dispense with the services of a personal trainer and design her own workout schedule with the help of the internet.

About three weeks into her sculpting routine, her personal trainer, Elliot – with one "T" as he would make a point of telling everyone he was introduced to. On this Thursday, Elliot of the single T, did not waste any time in deciding that he would make a move on Ella. Buoyed with misjudged confidence, his touches and nudges grew increasingly intrusive as far as Ella was concerned. His services were terminated abruptly one evening when Ella had had enough of her unwelcomed Lothario and strategically dropped a 20-kilo weight on his abs. A few inches lower and Elliot would have been contemplating an alternative line of work. Elliot with one T got the message and would not bother Ella again.

As Ella positioned herself for her first lift that would contribute to maintaining her admirable physique, a figure dressed in a striking black gym attire caught her eye. "Mmm! Fit," Ella reasoned, eyeing up and admiring the woman's toned body, perfectly flat stomach, and chiselled glutes. It wasn't unusual for Ella to eye up other women in the gym; these random gazes were a sort of visual barometer for the type of look Ella imagined for herself. She didn't want a muscled torso that bulged, she enjoyed the soft curvaceous texture of her body: she looked satisfyingly at the reflection of her own image in the mirror, happy with what she saw. "A runner doesn't need to put on too much muscle," she said, twisting left then right as she examined herself from every angle. Her mind returned to the weights waiting to be hauled up and pushed back down. "Four, five, six... One more set." But before she settled herself to complete her lifts, the "fit" figure in black attire crossed her eye line. She was familiar, but Ella could not place her or recall where or when she had seen her fellow gym bunny.

As Ella left the gym and headed for the DLR back to Lewisham, she quickly searched through the Rolodex of her memory for the person she had happened upon at the gym, but search as she liked, neither a place nor a time would jump up from her memory banks. The fleeting meetings, the snatched glances on the train while travelling to her office, or even the busy bazaars she would frequent when she had nothing else on the agenda, offered up nothing. There was no recall at all of the person she had seen.

"How was the gym?" Ray bellowed before he was properly in the flat. "Fine," was the response. Ella and Ray had an ongoing routine whereupon every Thursday of late nights and gym visits, Ella would stay over, usually getting in before Ray. "What's new," she asked. The inquiry was one of those questions that didn't always have an answer, but sometimes, those times when you can sense that something is needing to be said, the question would hang in the air like a rancid smell waiting patiently to be dealt with.

"Well?" asked Ella. "The usual nonsense," Ray said. "Usual? There is nothing usual about the work that you do, Ray." While the role as a police forensic photographer was always interesting, the grime under the fingernails of London's subterranean alternative reality of gang violence would often leave Ray emotionally exhausted. A tiredness that came from the Man Dem Crew over there having a disagreement with the E22 Lads over here, a perceived slight on social media - and another family is wrecked by the unnecessary grief and pain they must suffer because of the unwelcomed pain handed out by the nihilistic actions of the gangs.

The "usual" on this Thursday evening, though, was less gruesome than other evenings. "Two boys got into a scrap because one boy tried to mug the other boy for his expensive and exclusive designer trainers, only to realise at the last minute that the would-be victim was not alone and his mates were just a short sprint away," recalled Ray.

"The poor startled sod couldn't run away fast enough, and the boys stabbed him in the right thigh five times to teach him a lesson, apparently, though I'm not sure what that lesson is exactly," Ray said.

"You were about to tell me about your session at the gym?"

Before Ella could answer, the doorbell rang. It was Paul, just dropping in, as he does from time to time – unannounced and on this occasion, and unbeknown to him, unwelcomed. "Sorry mate, I didn't realise you had company, just thought you'd wanna neck a few beers," an apologetic Paul spluttered on seeing Ella. "You should've called," Ray said.

"Look, erm… I'll come back another time, I don't want to cramp your style, mate… three is an odd number, after all."

To Ella's relief, Ray's disappointed friend turned on his heels, uttered more barely convincing apologies and left the couple to their evening. "Is Paul OK?" asked Ella.

"S'pose so," Ray replied without giving Ella's question any real consideration.

"He looked disappointed," observed Ella.

"Yeah! S'pose he was."

The next morning Ella made her way down to the train station. She preferred the journey into Canary Wharf from Ray's flat because the transport links were so much better, quicker, and more convenient, not to mention, the fare was a tad cheaper. If she missed a train, she knew the longest time she'd have to wait was five minutes, whereas from her local station, she'd have to add another 20 minutes on to the waiting time and ultimately, the journey time. As she fumbled for her Oyster card in her voluminous bag that had a compartment for every occasion and possibility, she was gripped by mild panic. She searched the make-up pocket. Nothing. She scrambled around the spare change compartment. Nothing. For the third time, she prodded about where she keeps her keys, and where she normally placed her Oyster card. Nothing. It was then that a thought, as fleeting as it was disturbing to her, flashed into her mind, that maybe, just maybe, someone had taken it from her bag; it was, after all, left by the front door in Ray's flat. "No," she thought, "don't be ridiculous. He wouldn't dare."

Woman In Black

Michelle Stewart sat in the imposing lecture theatre of her university. The invited speaker was from an art-based collective called Londonmania that is in the know about all there is to know about England's capital city. The gist was that the language of the city ebbs and flows like the river that cuts through its heart. "English is an evolving language," the guest started, quoting from the blurb on their website. "Your class can also be determined by your language..." Michelle listened intently, her concentration every now and again drifting from the carefully constructed words of the language expert to the hem of her black, fitted dress. A thread had become loose. It was irritating her. Michelle liked everything to be in place. How was it that she didn't notice the offending loose thread this morning when she carefully laid out her lacy black matching lingerie, her black beret and her comfortable black shoes that was an impulse purchase while in Spain last summer. It was a trip taken on a whim as a reward for a tough term with her head locked in textbooks and balancing a master's degree with work, especially during a particularly busy period. The shoes were one of those purchases that was clearly a case of heartstrings battering the fiscal sense into submission. They were expensive, too expensive really, but Michelle's urge for the shoes calling her from the shop window was bordering on an almost primal need.

It didn't help that Frankie, her companion for the duration of her stay in Spain, a seemingly monied, native of Oviedo whom she had met during a previous long weekend trip to the capital of Asturias, Spain's rugged and verdant northern coastline, was all for the purchase. Frankie was a welcome bonus to the trip, not least someone to have dinner with. It was Frankie who selected the restaurant and recommended the fish dish, Merluza a la Sidra: *Hake in Cider*. The mules were also at Frankie's insistence. Michelle was partial to fish and reasoned that she was possibly in one of the best places to sample a top-notch fish dish. What she hadn't anticipated was that a small bone would lodge itself somewhere around her epiglottis, and no amount of water-gulping and back-banging from Frankie would move the stubborn obstruction, which would eventually loosen itself, much to Frankie and Michelle's relief. The offer from Frankie to treat Michelle was in fact a self-induced guilt offering after the pair had left the restaurant. Michelle, of course, couldn't resist the shoes nor Frankie's offer to pay for them.

The black leather mules with a slightly raised heel were a much-needed post-fishbone trauma pick-me-up as was Frankie. The pair would meet up whenever the opportunity arose, and this was one of those times when Michelle needed a break, and Oviedo offered culture, good weather and more importantly, a friendly face. The night after the evening of the fish incident, shoes in bag, Michelle gazed up at the stars from Frankie's apartment, where she was staying, and drank in the clarity of the skies, the chorus of cicadas and the tranquillity that the calming effect that her friend brought to the night, and sipped lazily and luxuriously, a good local red. At last, she could relax.

She slipped out of her loose-fitting black linen dress, climbed out of her black lace knickers, and liberated her firm breasts from the matching bra. As Michelle curled up under the cooling sheets, she felt Frankie's body slide in effortlessly beside her, caressing Michelle's toned back. They drew closer to each other, kissed slowly, deliberately and the two lovers meshed their bodies into a tight embrace. Roberta Flack's *The First Time Ever I Saw Your Face* played soothingly in the background. It was time for bed.

Michelle was jolted out of her intoxicating reminiscences by people shuffling out of their lecture theatre seats; she joined them and left the cavernous room. The lecture had raised as many questions as it provided answers. The talk had planted exploratory seeds, a need to learn more about the hidden lexicon of English: why do politicians talk in a learnt, coded way that appears only to resonate with their public-school peers? Why do young black men and women speak in such a fractured, disjointed, clumsy, inarticulate way? Correcting herself, Michelle reasoned that the disjointed, clumsy, inarticulate way in which London's youngsters - black and white - speak was most likely an assault on her ears only. To their peers, the disjointed, clumsy, inarticulate way of speaking was as normal as the latest grime or drill download streamed to their phone. Is there really much difference between the coded language spoken by the upper echelons of society and the more educationally disadvantaged, she wondered? She wanted a wider debate about the application and use of language and how it affords some people access to a wider society and stands in the way of others, and she knew who might fit the bill and provide her with some opinions, if not answers.

Michelle pressed Ray's doorbell repeatedly and with intent. The large front door swung open with force, the force of someone demanding to know who was so anxious to get his attention.

"Oh, it's Miss Black Beret," Ray said, "I thought you said you were going to call," Ray's voice dripping venomously with sarcasm and annoyance.

"Pleased to see you too Raymond," Michelle said, pushing her way past Ray and into his flat. "Do come in,"

Ray said, still holding on to the front door even though Michelle was by now in his front room and removing her beret and jacket, placing her bag carefully by her feet.

"I need your help," she said.

"For?" Ray asked, his annoyance subsiding after being reminded just why he was so attracted to Michelle after their previous meeting and why she had so intrigued him. Her attraction came from her gutsy, confident sassiness, he realised as he watched Michelle dominate the space that was but a few minutes ago, his, but now a space that had been skilfully and with aplomb, winched from his grip. "I trust you have coffee, Raymond. "Call me Ray." Stay where you are Raymond, I'll put some on." The imperative rooted Ray to the spot on which he stood as Michelle located the coffee maker and the Colombian medium roast in Ray's fridge and dexterously went about the business of showing her skills as a barista.

Michelle told Ray of her request, based on the logic that if he was interested enough in George Orwell, he must be interested in the overall role that language plays in how different strands of society communicate and its wider impact on the different communities up and down the country.

Ray, though flattered, hadn't given Michelle's appraisal of his academic credentials much thought; for him Orwell was just another representation of the country he had grown to love and now calls home. Nevertheless, he wanted to help, reasoning that language is nothing more than something that people use to communicate with each other. "In Jamaica, and across what used to be called the Commonwealth of Countries, the cosy family of like-minded colonial dependents, English was the dominant language," Ray reasoned, feeling that he had at least regained some control of the situation if not given Michelle a convincing insight to his heritage, a perceived advantage he wanted to press home to impress.

"Where I come from the English language conveys traditions and values and is directly linked to the Queen and Great Britain," he added.

"I didn't realise you were such a patriot, a torchbearer for queen and country," Michelle chimed in. "But do you think that language and how it is spoken among social groups acts as a sort of mates-rates acceptance badge into certain areas of society: an unwritten codex," asked Michelle.

Ray sensed that the woman in black who stood before him and gazed deeply into his eyes wanted to direct the debate to race, an idea he did not agree with, but did not know how to disagree with Michelle. Was he afraid of upsetting her? Of diminishing his importance to her. Was he, in fact, afraid of her confidence and assurance, or even afraid of her and intimidated by her? However, the thrust of her discourse surprised him. He realised that he was about to get a lecture on the pros and cons of race relations.

"Language is fluid and is not at all confined to ethnic groups," Michelle reasoned. "Rather, it is more defined by class. A poor working-class white person is as much at a disadvantage as the poor working-class black person... or any other poor working-class person, for that matter, if they cannot access the language of acceptance and inclusion that is normal among the ruling elite. Why is that? And how do we change that perception? And I can sense the presence of a woman in your flat, Raymond. I had you down as a single man on the lookout."

Ray fumbled, slipping and tripping, scrambling, and searching for a witty riposte. Nothing came. "Are you in love, or open to persuasion," asked Michelle. "I'm not fishing, by the way, you're not my type, though you could be with a strong following wind and in extenuating circumstances," she said teasingly, relishing the clear uncomfortable position in which she had deliberately placed Ray.

"Erm, err... language exists as a means of communication in a given community, that's why you have formal language and informal language; the way I speak to the officers at work is not the way I would speak to my mates, but does that mean that I have picked the lock of the barriers that exclude people like me from occupying the positions that are reserved for the top 10 percent of the population? No, it doesn't."

Michelle listened intently. "And the woman in your life?" she then asked. "Ella, her name is Ella and we've been together for a while now. She's great," said Ray, smiling. "Clever, understanding, loving, and she loves me as much as I love her."

"Mmm! That name sounds familiar, there aren't many Ellas around, and judging by her name she is English," stated Michelle. Ray immediately objected to Michelle's assumption, more in defence of his girlfriend's ethnicity than any possible comment on his choice of partner. "I thought you wanted to talk about the politics of language and not the politics of race," said Ray. Michelle sipped her coffee from her mug, cupping the large, porcelain vessel as she savoured the strong, luxurious aroma emanating from it.

"Shall we leave that one for another day Raymond? It's time I left anyway, thanks for your insights. I've taken up enough of your day and I have things to do, but I'll be back," she said.

"Back for..." asked Ray. "You'll have to wait and see," responded Michelle with a mischievous grin as she grabbed her black beret, her bag and headed for the front door. Before bringing the evening to a close, Michelle turned to Ray once more and said: "Race relations, though Raymond, we must get to the bottom of that sticky conundrum the next time we meet. You can't talk about Britain's class system without also addressing its rampant and ubiquitous racism.

Running Scared

The morning after Michelle had arrived at Ray's front door unannounced, Ella left her flat to run a few laps around Chalsey Fields, her local park, and had taken only a few strides when her phone rang. She didn't recognise the number so didn't answer the call. She instead slipped her phone into the pocket of her jogging bottoms, she set off, her first stride launching her powerfully away, the fresh air filling her lungs. She felt energised and quickly settled into a brisk pace. Soon her smooth skin glistened with sweat beads and her heart rate climbed as she pushed on. She was interrupted by her phone ringing again, the shrill repetitive chime breaking her concentration and causing her to slow her pace. It was then that she thought that she'd noticed an unfamiliar runner keeping perfect time with her strides – but from a distance. She increased her pace, but she sensed the pace of her shadowy accomplice appearing to match every increase in cadence, and any deceleration too. It was one of those occasions when one of her mother's proverbs could annoyingly burst forth in her consciousness. "You're always afraid of your own shadow...". She pushed her mother's emerging words from her mind before they could form and stopped abruptly, turned around to survey the scene and realised that she was alone. There was no other runner. No one was there. Had she imagined the whole thing? Shaken, Ella ran home as fast as she could, showered and headed to Ray's for their planned lunch.

Ella turned the key to her boyfriend's front door and let herself in before unleashing a giggly, throaty yell. Ray responded like an excited puppy greeting its owner who'd been out all day. They kissed and hugged – longingly and lovingly – Ray's comforting embrace washing over Ella like a protective blanket. Her world once more felt secure and assured, the events of the morning run pushed firmly to the back of her mind. She decided that she would not recall the events to Ray, reasoning that she does not actually have anything to share with him. It was probably all in her imagination, anyway. Over lunch Ella had checked her phone at least a dozen times more frequently than normal. Ray did not notice this increased fidget, and even if he had, he wouldn't have paid it much attention. Ray did notice, however, that Ella was not as talkative and opinionated as usual, even though the topic on the table of discussion was the previous night's latest TV thriller that had ended on a cliff-hanger. Television thrillers were usually a guaranteed invitation for an uproarious debate and exchange of opinion about the lead character or how contrived the plot was.

"What's up?" asked Ray. "Nothing, honest," Ella said rather unconvincingly. If she had given the same response to her mother, Ella, reasoned, there would be no hiding place. Nicola would have eked out the truth from Ella. Mother and daughter were as close as close could be. As a child growing up in their double-fronted Victorian house situated in Sidcup's more sought-after area, Ella was an unconfident child and turned to her mother for guidance as well as safety for most things. Sebastian, her brother who was two years older than Ella, blamed Ella for the fact that their father left the marriage. Rebecca, the youngest of the three siblings, was protected by the innocence of her age. Any damage that Stephen and Nicola inflicted upon each other washed over the young Rebecca. Sebastian and Ella, though, were less immune to the unravelling of their parents' marriage. To a 12-year-old Sebastian, it was easy to blame his little sister, who at two years younger, clung to her mother tighter than ever to shield herself from her brother's bullying and criticism. But she was old enough to question why Sebastian blamed her, but what she couldn't quite work out for herself was the truth, which was that their father left his young family after a year-long affair with his secretary was discovered when her daddy absentmindedly gave Ella his phone to play with. She was old enough, too, to know that the racy text messages that popped up while she was playing a game on her dad's phone one Sunday afternoon were not intended for her mum. Her mother knew at that moment exactly why her husband had been working late so often after Ella innocently handed the phone to her mother when her attention had been distracted by the children's show that had started on the television.

Sebastian conveniently blamed Ella for uprooting the close relationship he had with his barrister father. Sebastian blamed Ella, too, for the fact that he didn't go to private school like his sisters, but his parents knew from an early age that their less academically able son was not the type of student who would benefit from such an academically rigorous environment, unlike his studious sisters. When her brother left home to join the army as soon as he turned 18, Ella was beside herself with joy.

However, the absence of important male figures at such an early age began to impact on Ella as she entered university and adulthood. The framing of her understanding of the importance of a male presence had left Ella sensitive to the behaviour of men, and the experience had also given her an understanding of why men cheat. Her philandering father and her aggressive, bullying brother were placed permanently into a particular category by Ella. Trust was a difficult concept to easily accept; she could not help seeing a little of her father – will he cheat on me? – or her brother – will he undermine me; will he bully me? in every potential boyfriend that she met. The only constant was her doting, protective mother and her little sister who looked up to her and subconsciously absorbed the subliminal messages about the unreliability of men handed down by Ella, who later reasoned that it was this female-dominated upbringing that ignited Rebecca's interests in womanism and feminism.

Throughout lunch with Ray, Ella did not mention the running incident. After lunch, she thought that she should mention it, but decided against raising the topic of something that may or may not have happened for fear of not being taken seriously by her boyfriend. Ella ultimately decided that the phantom figure that was pursuing her on her run should remain a figment of her imagination. Ella felt that she ought to be able to confide in Ray, to be open about her feelings about any topic. Their relationship was becoming more serious, something that her mother had noticed - and unbeknown to Ella, it was something that her mother wasn't entirely comfortable with.

Mothers Don't Always Know Best

When Ella told her mother that she had met Ray and how she felt about him, Nicola had suggested caution given what she believed she knew about Jamaican men and their promiscuous reputation, their appetite for eyeing up women, smoking banned substances, drinking and partying. Ella closed her ears to her mother's warnings, rebutting her accusations as nothing but casual, unchallenged and unbridled racism, understanding that her prejudices were just that; prejudices founded on nothing other than what she reads in the Daily Mail and the neurotic fears of her churchgoing friends.

"Mixed-race relationships do not work," her mother stated as a fact. "Culturally people from the West Indies, Africa or wherever, do not share the same values as we do: food, religion, our history, a love of the countryside, books... you know what they say, if you want to keep a secret from a black man, put it in a book... they are not of the same class or education as us." By the time the last comment left her mother's mouth, Ella had heard enough of her blinkered and quite narrow thinking. Ella was disappointed in her mother because she had been raised to seek out and champion inclusivity, equality, diversity, justice and fairness in all people. Her mother did not recognise her own contradictions and her own jaundiced viewpoint as she spoke, but her words were not lost on Ella, who was now more determined than ever to show that all her points pertaining to Ray were in fact, the very same values that Ray had been brought up to believe in. They were British values that had been engrained after years of deferring to Crown and Country, to the British judiciary. Colonialism had its points; it could be argued.

The expectation of Ella's mother for her eldest daughter was for her to find a nice boy, settle down and get married. The expectation now that her daughter was in a mixed-race relationship was challenging for her mother. She began to question her own views and concluded that she may have to update her thinking in order not to upset Ella. The first step was to do what she had always done, which was to protect her daughter, and the second step, she decided, was to get to know Ray.

It was a task that she knew would take her a long time, despite her daughter's persuasive arguments as to the benefits of her new boyfriend. "Mum," Ella implored, "most men that I have met, men that would normally meet your approval, have not met my standards, standards taught to me by you, standards lived by your example."

"Yes, but…"

"But what?" Ella interrupted her mother sharply. "Let me ask you a question; or paint a scenario if you will. If Ray was blond and blue-eyed, would you feel the same way? Ray is educated, he has a good profession with the police, he is religious, though lapsed, he doesn't smoke, he doesn't do drugs, he doesn't sleep around, he is loyal, and he loves and cares for me, that ticks a lot of your boxes, yet all you can see is that he is black. Does that make sense, Mum?"

"No, but…" Ella's mother said, not offering a reasonable retort to her daughter's logic and the chastising of her entrenched views.

"…But Steve and you were such a nice couple," replied her mother. The statement was enough to bring up the bile in Ella, who then told her mother the truth of that relationship. Steve not only wanted a "skivvy" but someone who Ella could see was everything that she hated about her brother, Sebastian: the bullying, the goading, the having to come home and cook, clean and offer emotional and physical support. "I was dying inside, Mum. Steve didn't care for me and yet in your eyes he warranted the time that you gave him in deluding yourself that he would make a good husband and father. He was none of those things, he was manipulative, controlling and the years I spent with him were the worst years of my life, and you want to know why? Because I could see and feel my life slipping away from me, being squashed by this man who was stripping me of every ounce of self-worth that I had carefully built up since Dad left.

"I watched you struggle as I was growing up, and slowly I realised the emotional damage Dad had inflicted on you; and I was unconsciously choosing the same path for myself in the choice of partner: a man who would emotionally, psychologically, and spiritually abuse me, leave me feeling vulnerable and who knows, maybe he would physically abuse me too, given time. Steve was not the knight in shining armour that you like to make him out to be. He was slowly, ever so slowly, grinding me into the ground. I was like a piece of discarded chewing gum on the bottom of his shoes. Yet, you did not notice me shrivelling up, shrinking away, simply because he fitted a certain expectation that you had. You did not stop to ask yourself if he was right for me, was his behaviour, his values, his character suitable things that would have made you happy for me. Ray, though, fits another narrative, but not one that you can fathom or want to force yourself to entertain. Ray has more in common with you, me, your friends, your church group, and your way of life and your expectations than Steve ever will. It's bad enough that when we are out, we still get stares from black women and from white men, or from black men and white women. No one says anything but the subtle glances and the too-long stare is enough to tell me all that I need to know. What I don't need is the same shit from my own family. Your views are based on racial differences, Mum, which makes me question your emotional, spiritual and intellectual understanding of race, prejudice and racism. "

When Ella had finished venting her pent-up anger, her stunned mother stared silently at her daughter, the tears filling her eyes. "The noblest vengeance is to forgive Steve," her mother eventually uttered.

The proverb only served to rile Ella further. "Why should I forgive Steve, Mum?" Does he need forgiveness so that you and your friends and a wider society can feel better because forgiveness is a reason, they need to accept that I am sleeping with a black man. Should we not be beyond the point where we are dishing out this harsh judgement because of a person's ethnicity? And where do you suggest that I start looking to find Steve's finest qualities because I tried hard when we were together, and I failed to stumble upon one redemptive feature? I don't want revenge; I want you and society to stop judging me. I have been out with the monied City boys. No good. They arrive with massive egos that make them judge everything in material terms. I have dated the public-school type, who saw me as nothing more than eye candy. Ray sees me… the person. He doesn't judge me. He accepts me for who I am, not because I am this or I am that. My boyfriend is a decent man who just happens to have been born elsewhere other than within these islands, but he is a decent man. Steve was not a decent man, yet, somehow in your eyes, he is more suitable for me. Why?"

The exchange left Ella emotionally drained. Her mother's acceptance of Ray as her daughter's possible life-partner was for her, clearly still a work in progress. At that moment Ella needed someone to turn to, someone she could off-load her anxieties to, someone who would listen and tell her that everything will be alright, and that Ray is right for her, and that Steve wasn't right for her on any level. She didn't need a judgmental critic. Her mother could not see or accept Ray's obvious qualities because her views were blighted by the social stigma of being a single mother raising three young children on her own. To Ella's mother, the opinion of the community was important, therefore, the fact that her daughter had a black boyfriend mattered.

Ella's mother never told her friends why her marriage ended; such an admission would be tantamount to failure. Respectable, educated middle-class women do not become single mothers, or so she thought. The public knowledge of her husband leaving her and her three young children for a younger woman shone the spotlight on her perceived inadequacies, in her mind it would have made her look in the eyes of the other school-gate mums that she did not do what was necessary in a marriage to keep her husband. Shortly after Ella's dad abandoned the family home, her mother was consumed with doubts: "Was I glamorous enough? Had I put on too much weight after having the children? Did I satisfy him in bed? Why did he leave when I provided everything that he wanted"?

Mrs Somerton-Hughes had grown up in the seventies when the women's liberation movement offered the promise of equality – both politically and academically. The movement challenged the hegemony of male authority and the cultural and legal validity of patriarchy, it was a chance for women to feel free, to take control of their sexuality, their rights in the workplace, as well as in the home. Ella's mother, though, did not fully embrace the hopes of the women's movement, and although she engaged on one level, taking part in lively discussions around humanism at university, emotionally her conventional upbringing kept her from plunging head-long into the feminist movement. The break-up of her marriage and the circumstances surrounding how it ended caused her to hunker down and protect her children rather than face the wagging tongues and the accusative pointing fingers that would have labelled her a single mother.

When Ella was old enough, she realised that her mother could not rely on her father to be there for his family. At no time did she ever want to meet her father's new partner - the woman who had taken the place of her mum in her father's affections. Ella was also certain that Ray wouldn't let her down. He may need the occasional prod and push into action when he'd rather lounge in front of the television watching football, and she would have to bite her tongue on occasions so as not to tell him off when he hadn't done what she'd expected him to; like remembering to book a restaurant or buy cinema tickets in advance so that they'd be certain of seeing the latest film release, or securing the best table at a restaurant. But she knew that Ray's heart was in the right place, even if his intentions, away from work, where he was very focused and driven, were a little lackadaisical and fuzzy at the best of times.

While Ella was absorbing her mother's stance on mixed-relationships and her ill-informed assumptions about her choice of mate, Ray was busy fulfilling a previous arrangement with his friend. Paul was determined to catch up with his best mate, he wanted to see Ray on his own, when Ella was not around, like she had been earlier when he popped round unannounced to Ray's flat. Before Ella and Ray started dating, Paul would think nothing of stopping by Ray's. It was normal and habitual behaviour. The friends had arranged to go to a gig – at Paul's rather than Ray's insistence. The band was an up-and-coming quartet with a particularly striking lead singer, whose tight-fitting trousers was intended to ramp up as much sex appeal as a young man overflowing with testosterone could muster.

As the nubile lead singer let out the first note of the first song, his star appeal was immediate and evident. His alabaster skin made lighter by his jet-black hair and the intensely bright LED stage lights gave the young man clutching the mic an aura that his eager and submissive audience lapped up. "I told you he was good," said Paul. "And he's the group's main songwriter too… this number's about growing up without the love of his parents, feeling abandoned and all that emotional stuff. It's really deep and insightful."

"He's ok," was Ray's un-appreciative response.

The evening flew by in a whirl of song, sweat, beer and testosterone-fuelled sex appeal. Paul had been joined by a few of his musician friends, making Ray feel like a flat tyre on a clapped-out car. "Cheer up mate," ribbed Paul. "Not my type of music. I don't mind a bit of rock and roll but I prefer to stay in my little box of soul and reggae," Ray expressed, though Paul had heard this musical resistance from his friend a thousand times before. While they were at university Paul had tried to widen Ray's repertoire, extricating him from what Paul teased as his "musical cultural backwater". Ray, though, wasn't having any of it, sticking resolutely to what he had grown up with - a steady flow of Dennis Brown, Freddie McGregor, The Heptones, Shaggy, Luciano, Diana King and Capleton. Exposure to American soul music was as far as Ray was prepared to go to allow himself to explore a wider musical tapestry.

When Paul announced that he was leaving the gig with his musician friends who were going on to a private rave, and that Ray was welcome to come, Ray took it as a cue to head back to his flat. "Sorry Paul, I've got a busy working week ahead, don't want to lose any precious shut-eye." The two friends parted company, Ray heading for the last train back to south London while Paul headed further into the night.

Ray knew it was a mistake going out on the town with Paul on a Sunday night. He also knew that his in-tray was piled high with paperwork, mainly the laborious task of logging past cases. At work, he was hoping nothing new would come in as he waded through the mountains of paperwork. His wishes were dashed by late lunchtime when he was called to a job involving a stolen car, the type of supercar that caught the eye of two car-mad miscreants, and a car with a powerful engine – too powerful in fact, for the two 17-year-olds who decided that it would be fun, a laugh even, to steal the powerful beast and take it for a spin. Their adrenalin-fuelled adventure had ended abruptly when the driver lost control while taking a corner too fast. It took a series of street furniture that fell like dominoes, then a tree to bring the 3.5ltr motorised metal monster to a halt. It was fortunate no one else was involved. This fact no one else was injured was a circumstance of timing because the morning rush-hour had turned into a steady flow at the time of the accident. The occupants were bleeding and unconscious. The paramedics arrived just before Ray caught sight of the two youths being carried into the ambulance as he was climbing into his personal protection gear before dipping into his bag of tricks to record the gory mess of metal, skin and blood. "It's going to be another long night," he thought to himself.

It was the latest in a series of late nights and Ray was only too aware that he had not seen Ella as often as he would have liked. They spoke on the phone, but it was not the same. He missed her presence, her laughter, her ease. As a physical person, Ray was not comfortable with electronic means of communication: he preferred the intimacy of reading his partner's non-verbal communication, her gestures, and her glances. Eye contact was important to Ray. He made a mental note to make it up to the love of his life as soon as he could. Ella, though, had had other things on her mind that made her begin to question her actions, her movements, and her decisions, to be wary of the smallest little deviation that she could not make sense of. Her recent disagreement with her mother over Ray's ethnicity had shaken her and had left her questioning a relationship that previously she had no reason to doubt.

Ella arrived at her office still reeling from the fallout with her mother. She poured herself a coffee from the office filter pot, hoping it would be strong enough to blur her thoughts of uncertainty and help her focus on the clients that she had to attend to. One thing she could not afford to do was to have her personal concerns encroach on her professionalism. She had to make sure nothing was left to chance, the financial fallout of any mistake would be catastrophic – for her, her clients, and her firm.

It had been a busy day and Ella was glad when it was time to leave the case files behind till the next morning. The day had been stressful because she could barely keep her mind from going over thoughts of her relationship with Ray, and her relationship with her mother, both of which had always been rock-solid. She arrived home, walked slowly into her empty flat, removed her coat and poured herself a glass of wine before checking her phone for messages from Ray. The horribly inevitable response that she feared flashed up, the phone's black on white pixels left a sinking feeling in her stomach as she read: "Sorry! Won't be able to see you later – I need to work late again. Ray XX."

She paced around, chewing over the choice of cooking a meal for one or pouring another glass of wine. She settled for the latter, sat on the edge of her sofa and searched for reasons why Ray might have suddenly become so busy, so elusive. "Maybe he is having an affair," Ella wondered. The emptiness filled the room. It had been a week, or maybe just over since Ray and Ella spent any quality time together, just fooling around in their own company. "Anyway, who's counting how long it's been. It doesn't matter, really," she thought. But for Ella, it really did matter, but the emptiness continued to battle with her increasing insecurity. Ella questioned why the time goes by so slowly when all she wants to do is to press the accelerator and hurry things along to when she could be with her boyfriend without work getting in the way, a time when the next unfolding adventure could start, a time when their next embrace would lead to the next enthralling chapter in their developing relationship.

"I suppose I am busy too, but was I to blame? Or was it a collective subconscious agreement on both our parts, using work as an excuse. Is this how relationships end, with a gradual, subtle drift?" Ella wondered as the thought that Ray was perhaps deliberately staying away from her had entered her consciousness. She thought hard about their recent meetings. Volumes had remained unspoken, normally the pair exchanged an encyclopaedia of opinions, playful disagreements, furtive glances, snatched looks and laughter... each exchange echoing their love for each other. "If only I had said all the things that I wanted to say to Ray, things might have been different now," she remonstrated to herself. "I'll make it up to Ray when we next speak, I'll tell him exactly how I feel about him," she said, her mother's words nagging away at the pit of her stomach, all the time wondering if her mother knows best. "I'll make sure that I tell him exactly how I feel about him. Steve always used to say that I had a habit of putting my emotions safely away in a lock-up box. I couldn't speak to Steve, but Ray is so much easier to talk to. I won't be with Ray how I was with Steve," she vowed.

Ella's sense of balance, too, was put on hold, repeatedly telling herself that there was actually nothing wrong with her and Ray's relationship, it was just that their busy, complicated lives meant that they had to snatch at the gaps in their schedules whenever they could. She reasoned to herself that time spent together was fleeting for a reason, but to her at that precise moment, time seemed as elusive as trying to catch snowflakes on a winter's day. If Ella was here, Ray was there; if she was here, he was elsewhere… normally at some gruesome crime scene…. She longed for the day when their jangled misaligned lives would come together again, and to bring to a standstill the sliding doors of missed opportunities, to lose herself in the embrace of Ray's solid, strong arms. The doubts were taking root.

It could be another week or so before they would see each other again properly, work allowing, but in the meantime the emptiness that is taking up far too much space in her empty flat is somehow getting bigger, the absence of Ray's happy-go-lucky cheerfulness becoming more obvious. Ella felt alone. She decided that she would make good use of her time while Ray was busy working and read the many books that she had yet to plough through. Ella was an avid reader and had a habit of browsing bookshops and buying up to ten books on a whim. Her reasoning for her impulsive purchases was that she did not smoke, drank alcohol only in moderation and each month spent what she considered to be a small percent of her salary on clothes. A good read was her escape room, her bolthole for those times when she wanted nothing more than to hide away in a make-believe world when the real world was crowding in on her. She especially, too, loved the smell of the printed word on good, old-fashioned paper and not the nondescript glow of a digital readout that emanates from an e-reader. She favoured the tactile signals that came when paper came into contact with skin, the memories that the smell of a physical book would elicit.

An Unexpected Guest

The evening was balmy, summer was at its most beguiling, the smell of anticipation, of parties, of long walks by the river or in the country, and wiling away indulgent hours with friends, permeated the air.

While Ella was losing herself in a book, Michelle had arranged another visit to Ray's flat. As Ella turned the pages of the latest thriller, Michelle was knocking – loudly and persistently – on Ray's door. "Great! It must be Ella," Ray said to himself, bouncing up from his sofa and switching off the football on the TV. He could not hide his surprise and disappointment as he opened the door to the black beret-wearing Michelle who greeted him with nothing more than a nonchalant hello.

"Where's your princess, Raymond? Not entertaining you this evening," asked Michelle without a care if Ray's girlfriend had indeed been at her boyfriend's flat. Michelle had tried to recall where she had heard the name Ella before but still could not place her at a time nor place. She once knew someone called Ella but she couldn't be sure if it was the same Ella she had known in primary school. It was possible that she was completely mistaken. However, she reasoned that if Ray's girlfriend was not the same person she had met more than 20 years ago, then she would represent nothing more than an inconvenience; another potentially jealous woman who she would have to navigate around to get what she wanted, which was in this case nothing more than the perspective of someone who was a child of the Commonwealth. What was not apparent to Ray was that his guest was not thinking along the same lines as he was. For Michelle, despite what Ray had imagined, her manoeuvring and playfulness was not leading to a sexual encounter. It was not part of her intent.

Michelle's opening gambit caught Ray by surprise. "Orwell's book, you know, the one that brought us together," she said. "Well, Raymond, I was at a lecture the other evening and I want to get your opinion on something that Orwell wrote and resonates with my thinking on the politics of language." She cleared her throat and rustled around in her shoulder bag, retrieving a piece of lined paper and started to read: "*Most people who bother with the matter at all would admit that the English language is in a bad way, but it is generally assumed that we cannot by conscious action do anything about it. Our civilization is decadent, and our language must inevitably share in the general collapse. It follows that any struggle against the abuse of language is a sentimental archaism, like preferring candles to electric light or hansom cabs to aeroplanes. Underneath this lies the half-conscious belief that language is a natural growth and not an instrument which we shape for our own purposes.*"

"That's Orwell talking about language," Michelle said.

"I figured. Your point?" replied Ray.

"It's the last part that really grabs me, when he talks about language being an instrument which we shape for our own purposes. I believe that what Orwell meant was that language is used by the upper classes to maintain power over the working class. Language is liberating and emancipating. But those who cannot access language are bound, trussed up like a turkey, as if they had iron manacles around their ankles – and this is true for working class black kids as it is for working class white kids. I need to complete an assignment on how language imprisons as well as liberates us and I'd like to discuss it with you for your ideas – especially as you're an immigrant who has had to negotiate language to get on, yet you can easily slip in and out of different cultures and different classes - and different dialects when it suits you. See. Liberating. And where's your English Rose? She fascinates me - although I've probably never met her."

Two thoughts flashed through Ray's mind. He immediately wondered why Michelle held a fascination for Ella, and whether he agreed with her summary of Orwell's words.

"Language is about class, not race. Where I come from the middle classes are just as mobile and fluid as the middle classes in the UK, and it is your class status that gives you that freedom of movement. In Jamaica, the same differences that are apparent in that society are also apparent in this society. Even racial differences are apparent, but in the Caribbean, it is based more on shadism, rather than ethnicity, which in itself is historically entwined in racism - just look at the past Prime Ministers of my island - all white till the 70s, and all you have to do is look at the battle to get black cricketers to represent the West Indies. The struggles Clyde Walcott, Frank Worrel and Everton Weekes went through for cricket…. Their struggles to integrate the West Indies team were not dissimilar to the political struggles that society went through too. They are as much about race as they are about class, so you can't separate the two. And Ella's at her place. Why?"

"I'd like to meet her. I think I may know her, albeit from a very long time ago. Tell me about her."

"I thought you wanted me to tell you about Orwell."

"That can wait. I want to know what a fine-looking, fit black man sees in a white woman who I can only assume, if it is the same Ella that I am thinking of, is a rung or two above you in the class stakes, which also means that her family is richer than yours too. Tell me Raymond, is she lowering her standards for a chance to test the Mandingo Theory?"

"Mandingo Theory?" asked Ray, his face contorting in confusion.

"I don't recall George Orwell's discourse on that particular theory. Enlighten me."

"No, it's not one of Orwell's theories, but a long-held theme throughout twentieth-century literature – even Shakespeare touched on the subject in Othello: the brave, strong, love-struck soldier who is ensnared by the fair Desdemona. You know, that well-worn but persistent discourse of the sex-obsessed, well-hung black man deflowering the fair maiden. Is Ella your Desdemona, Raymond?"

"Isn't that racial stereotypical tosh," retorted Ray. "As I said, class is the defining feature of mixed couples, not race. If Ella were black or if I were white, we would still share the same passions, the same aspirations, we would still be together as a couple, we'd still be in love. Where I come from, we tend to judge people on who they are rather than what they look like – well, the educated class does, though I can't speak for some people who live in districts like Tivoli Gardens and similar areas where the overriding concern is what is allowed and not allowed by enforcers like the Water Lane gang - not race or class."

"Is Ella your Desdemona, Raymond?"

Michelle's persistent questioning began to irritate then anger Ray. He felt a growing and urgent need to continue to convince his black-attired tormentor that class and not race is the determining factor in mixed-race couplings, but he gave up exhausted by the realisation that this was not an argument that he was going to win.

"Look Michelle, like-minded people irrespective of colour will mix and socialise in London and most other large cities, and it is society's outdated conventions that deem it a problem when people from different races date or marry. In modern multicultural Britain, there is less of a pressure from some quarters of society that objects to the notion of miscegenation, those same notions that can be exacerbated when the pressures of class, career and friends are unreasonably exerted on such relationships. But those whose social status is less secure will congregate among their own and not break out of the comforting social confines of what they find familiar and comfortable. Mine and Ella's relationship is typical of the easy, meandering, interchangeable way in which many people live their lives today. Out Of Many, One People, is the motto of Jamaica, and I believe that to be true."

Ray smiled broadly, congratulated himself on his erudite summation of modern Britain, and continued to pontificate the subject of language, race and class with Michelle until she noticed that the time on Ray's digital clock was saying 11:45; a point in the evening, Michelle reasoned, that she should call a halt to the debate and make her way home. She had stayed much longer than she had intended and did not want to give her guest the wrong impression. "It's late Michelle, how will you get home, the bus that goes in your direction will probably have stopped running by now." Ray's rather obvious statement was more an opening gambit in a game of bedroom chess than a concern for Michelle's travel plans at this late hour.

Ray was still unsure what to make of Michelle. He stared at her while she gathered her belongings, not deviating his gaze from her svelte figure and not allowing her busyness to derail his one-track mind. As Ray ogled Michelle, he tried to understand her motives. "She's bold, certainly - sexually ambiguous - definitely. Was she after a one-night stand, a bit of fun maybe? Was this whole intellectual exchange nothing more than a conduit through which she would check me out? And does she want to know about Ella so that she can gauge her potential opposition's reaction should anything sexual happen?" Should it come to that, Ray knew that he would have to resist every manly instinct and pledge his love and loyalty to Ella.

"You could stay over if you want, you could sleep in the spare room, it's cosy and it is there for that purpose," Ray said.

"The spare room Raymond?" Michelle came back. "Why are you banishing me to the spare room Raymond?"

It was a rhetorical question, but Michelle calmed Ray's growing nervous uneasiness and dialled the number of her regular cab service. The journey home was a matter of a few miles. Ray was still trying to figure out Michelle's true intentions when she arrived at her Greenwich flat, threw off her clothes and her shoes, showered slowly and fell into a deep sleep - in her own bed. Any thoughts of Ray's offer of staying over had long disappeared, if indeed, they were there in the first place. Michelle was a woman who knew what she wanted and when. She always retained control of the situation.

The next morning a few miles away from where Michelle had fallen into a satisfying slumber the night before, Ella woke up early with the intention of resuming her runs around the local park. She was determined not to allow the events of two weeks before curb her activity, especially as running was something that she enjoyed and looked forward to. Ella tried to run three times a week – normally twice in the evenings after work and if she was lucky and wasn't too busy – again at weekends. Running was to her more than just a form of exercise, it was also a way to clear her head, to de-stress while getting a necessary dose of nature's goodness, which was essential for her all-round mental and physical health. Her place of work provided all the stress that she wanted, which meant her runs were more meaningful, and she wasn't going to let anything or anyone stop her from exercising. Running also helped her to cope with all the uncertainties that she had had thrown at her over the past few months, each one gathering into a bigger, unmanageable problem.

She sprinted away from her front door, not daring to look behind her, the memories still playing clearly in her mind of what she thought she'd seen and heard the last time she went out for a run. She galloped up the short, sharp incline of the entrance to the park, turned briskly into the left turn and glanced over her shoulder and slowed her pace in anticipation. Nothing presented itself. No one was there stalking her, threatening her sanity. No one was running behind her. She lengthened her stride, picking up the pace. Still nothing. Her muscles eased and her shoulders became more relaxed, and she focused on the cadence of her stride until she was back home, pleased that her routine had not been uninterrupted by something that she may or may not have seen on her previous run.

Ella had planned to meet Rebecca after lunch for their gym session. The two sisters were close. While at school Ella would always look out for Rebecca, especially when she joined her at her fee-paying school. At home they would chat endlessly, as sisters do, gossiping and giggling about anything that came to mind. This sisterly interchange continued as they grew into young women, though now the chatter was usually around the latest gossip about boyfriends and celebrities on social media. Rebecca looked up to her big sister and would do anything for her. Rebecca was in the final year of a postgraduate course in journalism and was in the comfortable position of not having to worry about money, an arrangement that was courtesy of a trust fund that was set up for the girls and their brother by their grandparents. This allowed Rebecca to focus on a writing career. Rebecca had a driving interest in modern feminism, and she particularly wanted to advance the arguments around the subject that was given prominence by the big thinkers such as Germaine Greer, Angela Carter and Mary Wollstonecraft. But that wasn't enough. Rebecca wanted to present an alternative, more progressive voice to feminism and counterculture as seen through the eyes of Lady Gaga, Malala, Geena Davis and Kathleen Hanna, and one day perhaps have her own name mentioned in tandem with the modern thinkers. Rebecca had lofty ideas about using her privileged education, not to perpetrate the class system, but to live and breathe in an atmosphere of ever-evolving ideas.

Lunch of avocado and smoked salmon on toast provided the fuel they needed before a workout, with a homemade protein shake for their post-workout pick-me-up. A Pilates class was booked, and Ella and Rebecca made sure that they were early for what was a popular session, which was due to the expert delivery of Simona, an enthusiastic and enigmatic teacher from Italy who put the class through its paces. As they completed the last stretch to end the physically taxing session, the two sisters collapsed into the comfy sofa in the chill zone area of the gym.

Ella and Rebecca chatted excitedly after the class had finished, both reflecting on a great workout that left them feeling exhausted but equally energised and refreshed. Rebecca, though, could not help but notice that her sister was distracted by the toned woman working out on the leg machine. "What's up," asked Rebecca.

"I know that woman, the one dressed in black leggings and the black crop top, but I don't know where I know her from," Ella said.

"Maybe she's checking you out, you have been staring at her, you know, and who knows, she might like what she sees," laughed Rebecca. As Rebecca and Ella made their way home from the gym, Ella confided that she was feeling unsure about her relationship with Ray and their mother's misgivings based on the fact that he's black and from the Caribbean, and that she was beginning to question herself, her sanity, recalling for Rebecca the missing Oyster card and the phantom jogger.

"Sometimes I think I am going mad. Without warning, everything that seemed secure now seems fragile and brittle, as if everything was built on a sandy foundation. Ray is always working, and yes, I know that job isn't a routine 9-5, but we just don't seem to spend as much time together as we used to. And Mum has really rocked my sense of balance. I hate to admit it, but what she said has affected me, it shouldn't, but it has, and it isn't something that I can easily put behind me. What shall I do, Becca?"

Rebecca's response was exactly as Ella had expected. Rebecca was a glass-half full type of person and always looked on the bright side of any situation, regardless of how dire it really was. Her job now as a sister was to reassure Ella that she wasn't being pursued by an axe murderer. "Ella, Halloween is a good few months away and a misplaced Oyster card is not an indication that you are losing your mind." Ella wasn't convinced that everything would be fine. Rebecca, though, was not persuaded by her own reassurances. She knew Ella better than most. With only a few years between them, the two women had navigated the choppy waters of adolescence into the chaotic hormone-induced teenage years arriving at a position where they were two sensible, grown-up young women. Rebecca could tell from her body language that Ella was not at ease, her demeanour had obviously become discombobulated, but she did not know what to do about it. Yet, she saw the danger signs in her sister's mental state. What she knew, too, was that Ella needed a shoulder now more than ever.

"Ella, whatever is troubling you, you shouldn't store it up inside otherwise the worry will eat you up. If you really are worried that things are falling apart around you all at once, do what you've always done: write a list of pros and cons, that way you can evaluate your situation. But personally, I think you've nothing to worry about. Let's catch up in a few days to see how you feel about everything then."

The weekend flew by and before Ella knew it, it was Monday morning and all she had to look forward to was another week of spreadsheets and managing the portfolios of the well-off. She would often wonder what rich people do with their money, and vowed that if she ever found herself in the position where she did not have to worry about the next pay packet, she would donate a sizable chunk of her earnings to a worthy cause. This particular Monday morning, lunchtime could not come around quick enough. She decided that a takeaway and a coffee, eaten out in the open, was the perfect antidote to a full in-tray. In the corner of her eye, and between mouthfuls of her pre-prepared meatless sandwich that was filled with too much mayonnaise, she was surprised to see the woman from her gym walk past.

"Excuse me," she cried after the high-heeled Adonai. "I know this is going to sound ridiculous, but I think I know you, well, I don't really know you but I have definitely seen you before, I think we've met before but I don't know where, or, rather, I can't remember where we've met." Ella had managed to stumble and trip her way through her clumsy introduction. "I'm Ella," she eventually said, still holding her half-eaten sandwich in one hand while balancing her coffee in the other trying not to spill the hot brew.

Michelle did not answer as she eyed up Ella from top to bottom. When the words did form, her response surprised Ella. "No, I don't think I know you. Have a good day." Before Ella could respond, Michelle had turned and was striding through the lunchtime throng of office workers and heading back to her desk and the awaiting in-tray full of insurance claims to wade through. "That went well," Ella reflected with a touch of self-deprecating sarcasm.

"So, the girl I knew at school is indeed Raymond's English Rose. Small world." Michelle whispered to herself as she opened the next case file.

Ella reached for her phone and dialled Rebecca's number eager to recount the awkward encounter. "Hi Becca, you know that woman we saw in the gym the other day, the one that you said I kept staring at, the woman dressed all in black? Well, I just saw her while I was eating my lunch, or rather stuffing my sandwich down my throat in the most undignified way. I made a complete ditz of myself by rushing up to her – she was all perfect and poised, of course – and blurted out that I know her, or rather I think I know her. She must have thought she had been accosted by a street beggar or something. But before I could explain myself, she just left. Turned on her expensive high heels and disappeared into the foreground. I felt stupid…. Rebecca, are you there?"

Ella had been talking ten to the dozen, not allowing Rebecca to interrupt the conversation with neither question nor comment. "Yes, I'm still here but I was trying to find an opportunity to say something, but you kept blabbering on. Well, who is she?" Annoyingly, all Ella could say was "I don't know." She could not provide an answer for her sister's question. However, with dogged determination, every lunchtime for the next two weeks Ella strolled up and down the open area of Canary Wharf where food vendors sold their lunchtime offerings and eager workers headed for the Underground at clocking-off time, mixing among the bankers and the brokers in the hope that she would see Michelle again. Through her third-floor window that afforded a clear, panoramic view, Michelle, though, had been watching Ella stroll agitatedly up and down each lunchtime, watching her every move, calculating a time when and how she would remind Ella that they had met in primary school, while at the same time wondering why Ella was strolling in what appeared to be a wayward fashion.

Michelle's lunchtime non-appearance bothered Ella somewhat, to the extent that when she had arranged to meet Ray and Paul after work, an arrangement arrived more at the persuasion of her boyfriend than any initiation on her part. While caressing a large glass of Pinot Noir, but not enjoying it, it was clear to Ray that Ella had other things on her mind. Paul, too, must have sensed her unease, glancing at Ray he pointedly asks about Michelle, though he did not mention her name. The casual inquiry piqued Ella's curiosity. "Well, have you seen Mystery Lady," Paul said teasingly. The question wasn't lost on Ella who wondered if Mystery Lady could be the same woman at the gym, the same woman who works probably no more than a few feet away from her. Ella was already racked with uncertainty about, as far as she was concerned, her faltering relationship and her unbalanced state of mind that any mention of another woman would set her confidence on a downward slide. The journey home was unusually quiet. The usual chatty exchanges and the laughter between Ray and Ella was muted. As they entered Ella's flat, Ray held her gently around her waist, pulled her towards him in anticipation of a kiss, or at least a warm embrace.

"What's bothering my girl," he asked.

She pushed her boyfriend away and asked: "Do you still love me, Ray?"

It wasn't the response Ray had expected. "Who is Mystery Lady? Why did Paul ask you about another girl while I was there? It seemed like a deliberate, provocative act of attrition. What is he trying to imply, Ray? What am I supposed to infer from his troublemaking?"

Ray was genuinely lost for words. To him, Michelle was nothing more than a curiosity, a coquettish flirt, but nonetheless, someone, Ray reasoned, that he was happy to help because she appeared harmless in her enthusiasm to share academic discourses with him. Ray no longer saw anything ulterior in Michelle's intention and could not see that he could be doing anything other than being his typical, accommodating, helpful self.

"I will ask you again, Ray. Are you seeing someone else? Do you love me." Ella projected her voice to give off the confidence and certainty of a woman who was willing to fight for the man she was in love with. However, the strident delivery was all she could muster to fight off a growing fear that at any moment that same strong, projected voice would crack and falter, become frail and crumble with uncertainty and weakness. Doubts had been raised on a previous occasion when she first met Ray's parents, Ella remembering their courteous but less than enthusiastic welcome into their lives that she had received. They were too polite to voice any concerns, but Ella was aware that what her Englishness and her class represented to Mr and Mrs Gordon was their son crossing the tracks, dating out of their comfort zone. But in this instant, it was not the time to show weakness, to have her mother wheel out another one of her proverbs that would probably go along the lines of "I told you so; those who can't hear must feel". She did not want to hear the muffled sniggers of her so-called friends who had stopped calling her as regularly as they once did since Ray and her became a devoted couple, it was not the time to get a lecture from her brother on one of his weekend visits home while rejoicing in the news that her black boyfriend was seeing another woman behind her back.

"Ray, I spoke to Rebecca about the weird things that have been happening to me, and the fucked up way my mother turned the tables on everything that she raised me to believe in and questioned if you and I were right for each other, despite the fact that when she sees you, she's as lovely as ever. But, If I'm to be perfectly honest with you, Ray, I asked Becca if she believed that Mum had a point. So, yes, I am beginning to question what we have. We live in an age of supposed enlightenment, we are all supposed to know better, and we live in one of the most diverse capital cities in the world when these things shouldn't matter. Racial prejudice, I believed, had been consigned to the dustbin of history around the time that Tony Blair and New Labour came to power to usher in a new dawn, a society where Cool Britannia ruled, but it hasn't turned out like that, has it? Blair was a huge disappointment and we seem to have taken massive steps backwards; what should be important is that people see people as they are, not what they look like, and all the prejudices that go with that messed-up attitude.

"My sister has always been there for me since we were little, and she is supportive in everything that I do, she champions our relationship, she hasn't once gone dark on me because you and I are dating. But I need reassurance, I need to know if you are messing around, Ray. Rebecca reminded me that while growing up - and she has lived every page of my short and unexciting love life with me since - I have been particularly choosy when it comes to men. Yes, I may have made a few duff choices – Steve springs to mind – but generally my instincts are sound. So, Ray, I need some answers from you. Now!"

Ray knew that the time had come for him to explain himself fully, to remove any doubts in his girlfriend's mind. He didn't, after all, want to lose her. He had spent a lot of time and emotion nurturing what he had always wanted: a woman with whom he could be proud of, a compassionate, understanding, uncompromising, honest partner that he could love - unconditionally. They collapsed into the soft, comfortable sofa with the joint intention of clearing the air, which crackled with tension. After two hours of explaining who Michelle was and the circumstances of how they met, Ella understood and was reassured that she was not such a mystery lady after all, but a fictitious femme-fatal that Paul had mischievously put among the pigeons. Michelle was not the person who was trying to wreck her relationship with Ray.

Paul, Ella reasoned, was disturbed by her, though he might have had his reasons, he couldn't articulate them and any attempt at a plausible explanation were flimsy at best. Paul remembers the first time that he met Ella. It was soon after Ray had introduced him to her. An evening on the town had been planned and Ray thought that it would be fun to invite his friend and his new love to a gig. Ella, though, turned down the offer on the reasoning that she did not feel secure enough in her developing relationship with Ray to avoid feeling like a spare part to the two pals who'd known each other for what seemed like forever. However, Paul made it clear that he had felt snubbed and had misread Ella's apprehension as an attempt to sidestep him. It was a flimsy reason to take a dislike to Ella. But he did. Paul could not take the perceived rejection and reasoned that Ella being with Ray was nothing more than sexual curiosity underpinned by power and oppression. Paul never made his feelings known to Ray, reasoning that his friend was only with Ella because he viewed black women as overweight, poorly educated and lacking in social finesse. Paul convinced himself that Ella was just another middle-class woman dipping her toe into the very small pool of black men who are educated and cultured, who are devoted and loyal and who take their career seriously – and they would then dump them, never brave enough to prolong the relationship to a point where they are introduced to her family and incorporated into her world of privilege. It didn't occur to Paul that he might be jealous of Ray, or that Ray and Ella's friendship had developed because they had a lot in common, shared similarities and they were together irrespective of their race and cultural differences. Paul was drawing on his own confused experience from his childhood that blurred his judgement where Ella was concerned. Paul also knew that by mentioning the possibility of another woman in earshot of Ella, it would tip her world into a tailspin. He was the fox in the chicken enclosure, and he was enjoying his predatory role, enjoying the fact that his instinctive but unfathomable dislike for Ella made her uneasy and uncomfortable. He wanted Ray and Ella's relationship to come to an end, he disliked the fact that Ella was dating Ray, but he didn't understand why. Paul was happy to inflict pain and uncertainty on Ella if he could avoid scrutiny and could skip away happily into a musician's world that was a merry-go-round of late nights, fun, hedonistic clubbing, music, and occasionally, the questionable acquaintance.

Ella thought back to the long air-clearing conversation she had with Ray, but despite his perfectly plausible explanation, there was a smidgen of doubt that remained. She was trying to make sense of why Paul saw fit to embarrass her in front of Ray by mentioning another woman, which made her more determined to find Michelle and speak to her to hear her version of events. If she was the other woman that was threatening her relationship, she would confront her, let her know that she will not allow her to come between Ray and her. She, therefore, made it her duty to find Michelle. During her all too short but precious lunch breaks, she spent the next week seeking out the immaculately dressed woman in black with the flowing locks. It was Friday, and Ella was still without the answers she was searching for: was her boyfriend telling her the truth? What is the real relationship between Ray and this so-called Mystery Lady? She was about to return to her office when she felt a hand on her shoulder. Ella swivelled round to find her face to face with Michelle. "I think you do know me, but you probably don't remember me. When you accosted me the other day you said you know me. I couldn't place you at the time, I could not clearly remember anyone called Ella. But then I remembered you from primary school. It was a long time ago, yes, but I recalled that you had a name like Eloise or Allison or Ali. But your name escaped me. Eventually Ella resurfaced in my memory banks. I suppose we should get reacquainted with each other, Ella."

Ella was stunned, but this time she was determined that she would remain calm and coherent. "I don't recall you from school, but I have seen you at the gym... we appear to go to the same gym. I've seen you working out. I have also seen you away from the gym, but I couldn't place the time or the occasion. But I know that I have seen you before. I live in Brockley; my boyfriend, Ray, lives in Blackheath and we often come down to Greenwich to socialise. Maybe we've met while on a night out."

The mention of the various locations, the fact that they attended the same primary school, and Ray's name confirmed to Michelle the fact that this was indeed Ray's English Rose. "It's good to see you again… Sorry, I don't recall your name."

"Michelle Stewart. I was in Miss Benson's class. You?"

"You look so different. I was in Mrs Bryant's class. I need to speak with you. We've a lot to catch up on. Can we meet tomorrow, at the coffee shop in Greenwich Church Street? I'm sure you know it: it's practically next door to an old book shop called Taylor's. Will 12-noon be ok?"

At the mention of the name of the dusty bookshop, Michelle's mind flew back to the time when she first met Ray and their comical but flirty exchange over Orwell's book. She remembered, too, the look that the woman she now recognised as Ella gave her as she left the bookshop. The memory of that fleeting meeting had lodged itself in Ella's recall, too, and she remembered Michelle as the woman who had been in conversation with Ray over a book. "Yes, that's fine. See you tomorrow." Michelle nodded in agreement.

Clearing The Air

Ella spent the evening and the next day in nervous anticipation of their arranged meeting. Life has a twisted way of placing all the cards in the wrong places. Was her boyfriend having an affair with someone she knew from primary school? She knew that she was potentially putting her hand into the hornet's nest. She knew, too, that she'd feel humiliated if Michelle admitted that she was in a covert tryst with Ray, if indeed, she'd even declare something as incendiary as that. Ella wondered, too, if by seeking clarity, she could find herself accusing another woman of something that she might be entirely innocent of.

Ella made sure she was early, she wanted to get a good look at her long-forgotten playground pal, and possible love rival as she walked through the door of the coffee shop. She felt a flush of nervousness as Michelle opened the door, scanned the room before finding Ella looking at her keenly.

"What are you having," Ella asked.

"Coffee. Black, no sugar, no milk," replied Michelle.

Ella noticed that Michelle takes her coffee the same way she does. The two women sat as far away from the busy tables of the café as was possible, both trying to seek out a quiet space. The awkwardness between them was a mixture of curiosity and intrigue. "I don't know how to begin, but I will just get straight to the point," said Ella. "I am suspicious that my boyfriend, Ray, is not being truthful or faithful with me, and while I am not accusing you, his best friend, Paul, a musician, asked him about a so-called "mystery lady" while we were out having a drink recently. I felt that his comments were designed to get at me. I confronted Ray about what Paul said when we got home, and he mentioned your name. It is just a weird coincidence that we share a past history and appear to work in the same cluster of office buildings and that I have seen you at my gym too. I think that Paul deliberately phrased his announcement the way he did because he has never been comfortable with the fact that Ray and I are dating. I don't know why he feels that way about me, but I get the distinct feeling that he'd rather that I was out of the picture. I find him slightly odd, If I am honest. His behaviour towards me does not add up."

Michelle sipped her coffee. Returning the cup to the sand-coloured laminated wood table, she raised her eyes to meet Ella's uncertain gaze before giving her side of the story. "I met Ray over a book that we both wanted, which we eventually agreed to share. I returned it to him a few weeks later. He's telling you the truth, but clearly someone isn't being as honest with you as Ray is. Look Ella, Ray is a cool, interesting, clever guy. He's cute too, but he's not on my agenda, so you don't have anything to worry about from me. My interest in Ray is purely academic. Let me explain. Although I work in insurance, I am studying for a master's degree in applied linguistics, which involves looking at language and how it is used in society and between the classes, how language is used as a tool for power and control. One day I hope to swap the boring old spreadsheets for a life full of words and idioms as a university lecturer."

Ella sat silently, listening intently to what Michelle had to say, feeling a bit of a fool, too, for making assumptions about the relationship between the woman in front of her and her boyfriend. She thought about apologising to Michelle and apologising to Ray too for doubting his story. "Michelle, I feel a bit of a fool now. Sorry! But some weird stuff has been happening to me lately, so much so that I am beginning to question everything."

The two women agreed to exchange numbers and before leaving the café they agreed to meet again to catch up on each other's life since school. "I live in Greenwich, and where do you live these days," asked Michelle. "Brockley, as I mentioned," replied Ella. "Lunch?".

"Yes, let's do that," Michelle responded.

Ella took a long walk through Greenwich Park, across Blackheath and on to Ray's flat. She was determined to spend as much time as she could with her boyfriend given that work had been taking up so much of his time of late. She climbed the stairs to Ray's front door and paused for a reflective moment. Will Ray fly into a rage because she took matters into her own hands because she had not believed that he had told her the truth, or would he just laugh it off as he laughs off most things. Nothing seems to upset Ray, not even something that could derail their relationship. "Typical," she thought, promising that one day she will push Ray out of his too laid-back approach to life. Ray let her in and was greeted by a contrite apology, explaining that she'd "met Michelle to clear the air, only to find that there was no air to clear, and by some weird coincidence, it turns out that we went to the same primary school".

"That was pointless, I told you all there is to know," Ray said, mocking the fact that Ella did not believe him. "Small world. It's an odd coincidence that you and Michelle went to the same school. Another thing, Ella, when will you get it into your head that I will climb mountains and swim oceans for you? I wouldn't lie to you. By the way, I have a visitor."

Ella heard a loud scream from the front room, her name being shouted at a decibel level that she was not aware was possible from a human. "Oh, hi Gerald," she said, giving Ray's big brother a warm hug.

Gerald took great pride in teasing Ella, picking up on the fact that she may not be feeding Ray in the way that he is used to, a clear reference to his mother's carefully cooked Sunday dinners, Jamaican style, so delicious that while growing up the brothers would arrange their social calendar around their mum's cooking, especially on Sundays when a plate of rice and peas and stew chicken would disappear and seconds and sometimes a third helping would be eagerly gobbled up too.

"Ella, Ray's losing weight, girl, you're not feeding him properly. Look, I'm going to personally take you to Brixton market one of these days to show you what he's missing. Ray, when did you last have some fried plantain for breakfast? Can she cook stew peas and rice?" Gerald let out a loud belly laugh, pleased at his own ribbing of Ella's perceived lack of ability and knowledge of Jamaican cuisine.

"Actually, Gerald, I do know the difference between a Julie mango, a common mango and a papaya, I can tell what is callaloo and what is spinach. You've obviously forgotten that I love cooking and love trying out different cuisines from various countries, and having a Jamaican boyfriend, it was only natural that I'd become interested in your country's cuisine, and If you were to come round more often, you'd taste my food, and my fried dumplings and plantains, ackee and saltfish – and hot chocolate, apparently the way your grandmother used to make it. So, Gerald, you'll have to find another line of mockery; you can't catch me out when it comes to cooking, and I have been going to Brixton long before I met Ray," she laughed. Gerald could not respond.

"Seriously, though Ella, what will you do when the rugrats come along – I trust I'm not being too presumptuous – but I have a mate whose wife, English, obviously, hasn't got a clue how to groom her kids' thick, tight, curly hair. She just leaves it to grow and when it becomes too much, she marches them round to her sister-in-law."

"That won't happen, Gerald, you know that, besides, you're making massive generalisations about us poor ill-informed white girls who snag your men and know nothing about their culture. What do you take me for anyway?"

"That's told me, then, hasn't it Ray. I'd better change the subject," Gerald retreated quickly, knowing when he had lost the argument.

"Don't bring me into this debate, it's between you and the good lady. I will say though, that you walked right into that one Gerald," Ray said. The three of them laughed uproariously before heading for the kitchen.

That evening, after Gerald had left, Ella returned to the subject of her meeting with Michelle, sharing with Ray what the two women had talked about. "I like her, she's very confident and is quite poised. We've agreed to meet again for lunch, and I am sorry that I doubted your intentions. But what I did share with her was something that I want you to clear up for me. I received a letter, posted to my home address. I showed Michelle the letter, but she said it was not her handiwork, which begs the question:

who did write it? I thought it would be odd if she had written the letter because she doesn't know where I live. Might you have an explanation, Ray." Ray began to read Ella's incriminating evidence:

In infinitum, without end, in perpetuum ... Feelings are always hard to express in words, they are often better when felt. Emotions are not tangible, tactile grabby things that you can hold in your hands; rather, they are a spontaneous smile, a lingering thought, a belly laugh, a touch, more purpose in the stride, and all brought on by you: your face, your smile, your smell, and the memories that you inspire.

Meeting you, Ray, has been the most exhilarating and mad thing that has happened to me for a long while. Do I feel eighteen again? Yes I do.

What I can't seem to describe with suitable and appropriate eloquence are the feelings: of aching to see you all the time, of sitting at home saying your name over and over - and smiling, of wanting to feel your strong, passionate embrace, of wanting to kiss you, of wanting to be with you, of feeling my skin tingle when I think of you, of ending each day satisfied knowing that you are in my life.

How do I feel about you? Hopelessly in your thrall, weak, eager, triumphant, excited, lustful, lovely, all out of sync, disjointed, renewed. You just make me feel. I have rediscovered feelings again. Put simply, I want you in infinitum, in perpetuum.

But there's Ella...

Call me on Sunday morning at precisely 11:06

Michelle

"Well, what do you make of it? Michelle clearly didn't write the letter, and the person who did went to the trouble of making sure that I read it. So, who wrote it? Any ideas Ray?" Her boyfriend could not offer a plausible explanation. "I don't know. It could be anyone, but it certainly wasn't me, that I am certain of," he said. The anonymity of the letter's author left Ella confused and concerned in equal measures. "So, if neither of you wrote it, then who did. Look, I have no idea where this has come from, but it is making me afraid. Should I go to the police, Ray? You work for the police, tell me what to do about this. Michelle did not have a suggestion when I asked her what to do about the letter that she was supposed to have written but didn't. I don't know what to do anymore, I don't know who to turn to feel safe. All I can feel is an emptiness, an ache in the pit of my stomach… and it feels like fear. It *is* the feeling of fear, and the worst part of it is that there is nothing either of you can do to stop it. And it is this crushing feeling of dread. I need to find out who the instigator of these threats is and stop whoever has apparently got it in for me."

Ella and Michelle kept their agreed appointment. The mood this time, however, was less awkward than their first meeting. "What happened to Sally? Do you remember her? All the boys used to tease her because of her ginger hair," recalled Ella.

"I have no idea what happened to her, and I used to get teased too because of my plaits, so I can only sympathise with Sally," laughed Michelle. "You used to hang around with a girl called Jayne. What happened to her? I suppose she's married with a litter of kids by now; she was always popular with the boys. Didn't you also have a little sister at the school?"

"Yes, Rebecca. I'm sure you'll meet her again, but she's very different from that clingy irritating kid who always stuck to me like an apron. She's all ballsy and grown up now, and full of forthright opinions." replied Ella.

The two women combed over every scrap of memory from their early years. However, the light conversation would change the mood to a more stressful tone when the chatter turned to the present day. Ella offloaded all her recent problems on to Michelle.

"Ella, don't cry. I can't begin to understand or know how you feel right now, but the pragmatist in me says that tears won't get to the heart of this; it won't get you the answers that you require. What we need is a cool head. Let's try and figure this out." Michelle's comforting words made sense to Ella. It was very unlike Michelle to reach out to a woman she hardly knew, but that shared beginning was all the bonding they needed. Female friendships can be hard-won, they have to be worked at, but there was something about the grown-up Ella that meant that Michelle felt at ease, and she let Ella into her usually fortress-like, guarded world.

Ella knew that she had to find out who was trying to ruin her life. She knew, though, that it wasn't Michelle, which made her feel more relaxed around her would-be adversary turned possible friend. Compared to their previous meeting, this time the nervousness and uncertainty that lingered had gone, replaced by Ella searching for answers as to who had sent the unwelcome letter. The uncertainty of what might be said and what is not known from what is known was no longer apparent. The two women had also established an uncluttered certainty that Michelle was not the femme fatale that Ella had first imagined her to be. Instead, Michelle proved to be an unlikely but welcome ally.

"Ella, whoever sent that letter knows where you live and has bad intentions for you. Can you think of any ex-boyfriends who might be stalking you? I know it sounds far-fetched but at this moment, I wouldn't discount anyone. Any crazy exes in your closet, Ella? Let's change the subject, but obviously we must get to the bottom of this, even if we take it to the police, they have to at least register it as a case of stalking - but first we have to find out who it is. But for now, let's get to know each other better, then you can tell me more about your troubling situation. How often do you go to the gym Ella? I make sure that I go at least three times a week. I feel out of sorts if I don't get my dopamine hit from pumping iron. I want to grow old disgracefully but with a great bod," Michelle laughed.

"I'm more of a gym newbie, running is more my thing. I find it liberating and relaxing. I see a gym session as a complement to my running. I'm just learning about what I'm supposed to do with weights. Maybe you can teach me how to lift as we both belong to the same gym."

Michelle liked the suggestion, but she wanted to find out more about Ella's predicament, not her gym habits. She did not waste time before starting to quiz Ella. She was keen to get back to the task of discovering who her possible stalker could be. "When we met in the café, you said that some weird things have been happening to you of late. What do you mean?" Ella recalled for Michelle the mysteriously lost Oyster card, the "ghost" runner and how she had been made to feel detached, questioning herself and her judgement after her mother's remarks about her previous boyfriends and how they might be more suitable as a life partner than Ray is. "She didn't say it, but I knew what she meant. My mother raised us – Rebecca, my brother and I – to be tolerant and not to judge, but it appears she is not prepared to live by her own beliefs when it comes to her own daughter. I have also had Ray ask me about things that he said that I supposedly said. These are things that he heard from Paul, and when I tell Ray I did not say anything of the sort, Paul apparently denies it when asked by Ray, making me look like a liar, even suggesting to Ray that I should prove that he said what he most definitely said.

"Such as…?" Michelle asked.

"Well, one day he turned up at my place of work for no real reason, though I don't think that he knew that I knew that he was there. He had the audacity to ask at reception if I was in and that he was a friend of the family and that he had a gift from my father that he had to get to me. Fortunately, the security at my office is tighter than GCHQ and when he was asked to leave the supposed package, he sheepishly declined and left - with the package carefully tucked under his arm. I really don't understand why he would think that I wouldn't learn about it."

"He meant for you to know. Is there anything else that he did?" Michelle interjected.

"Well, if you count the unwanted phone calls, the text messages, which were sometimes a rambling monologue of accusations that didn't make any sense to me but were nevertheless no less threatening and scary. I don't even know how he got my number. I just presumed that Ray gave it to him. And I haven't mentioned this to anyone, but he has followed me too, or he has "coincidentally" showed up unexpectedly at times and places where I wasn't expecting him. There was at least one occasion when he followed me, trying his best not to be seen, but I sensed that someone was following me and a fleeting glimpse in the shadow was enough to confirm that Paul was following me at a distance. I always made sure I was in a lit area when I made my way home and that there were other people around. I was such a nervous wreck, sometimes I don't know how I made it to my front door. The whole thing with Paul has left me shaken and has just added to my growing anxiety. I debated for ages whether to tell Ray what has been happening and how I feel, and when I did try to tell him, he laughed it off, not allowing me to finish and offering some lame excuse about Paul being absent-minded and prone to fantasies. I didn't think it was a laughing matter and I don't think it has anything to do with Paul being absent-minded, and I was disappointed with Ray's response... I expected more support from him, at the very least I expected him to listen to me and acknowledge my concerns. And when I happen to bump into him when Ray and I are together he would stare at me with what I felt were dark intentions... I would sometimes notice, I would catch his glare and he'd look away sharply, but he would allow his stare to linger just long enough in this threatening, suspenseful, controlling way... He wouldn't say a word. It was chilling. But Ray never noticed, he was oblivious to Paul's silent intimidation, but it is difficult to expect Ray to notice. There is no reason why he should, he is not the one who is on the receiving end of Paul's weirdness. But the thing is, Michelle, a few days ago, Ray, casually as he does, said he asked Paul about delivering something to me at work and Paul denied it. He lied! He lies in a really ugly way. He said he doesn't know what Ray was talking about. And Ray didn't question him, he just took Paul's word as gospel. He believed him ahead of me. How am I supposed to be reassured from that type of reaction from the person who is supposed to always look out for me?"

Michelle listened intently, carefully trying to make sense of Ella's torment. Eventually, she asked: "What's Paul's surname?" Ella replied: "Robson, or is it Robertson... something like that." Michelle remembered that Ella had mentioned that Paul was in the music business. The name sounded familiar to her. When she returned to her office, she retrieved all the names that sounded like the names Ella had mentioned. She counted on the possibility that she may have insured him in the past. A satisfying grin reshaped her soft features, turning concern into a smile when she pulled out the file labelled "Paul Robinson". "Ah ha! At last," she whispered to herself.

Ella invited Michelle to her flat to share what she knew about Paul Robinson. Ella had planned to cook a simple pasta penne dish with tomato and basil sauce, washed down with plenty of wine. "Is this your man? Paul Robinson, bass player, quite successful, plays bass with a lot of the best bands, does a lot of commercial gigs, but is a complete pain in the you-know-where for us to deal with because he never completes his forms on time and they are never filled out properly, so we then have to go the extra mile just to make sure that his expensive equipment is properly insured and gets to its destination without incident. I have met him probably no more than twice, and only in passing when he comes to the office to complete forms. It's obvious from the letter that he clocked who I was because he knows my name - and used it to bait you. Why is he harassing you?" Michelle asked.

"I don't know, I wish I did know. He clearly doesn't like me, but I don't know why he doesn't like me, but I need to know why before he ruins my relationship - and drives me insane at the same time. Maybe that's his plan. It's as if he's intentionally trying to get under my skin, to ruin me."

Michelle continued to divulge what she knew about Paul Robinson, expanding on the fact that when her company took him on, there was a series of questions that the underwriters wanted answers to before they would issue the policy. It is not unusual for companies to ask questions at the slightest hint of risk. And risk could come in the form of the most benign possibility.

"The fact that Paul Robinson's file had raised a few red flags, regardless of how minor, was enough for the insurance sleuths to start digging. He's an artist, as we label musicians, and artists are a peculiar breed; the best way to approach an artist is to believe that they are going to do something that is completely unexpected, they are without any sense of responsibility, all they care about is their art, and everyone and everything else can go to hell in a handbasket. He's been up to something, to that I am certain because of that little glitch in his file."

"What do you mean?" asked Ella.

"I don't know. I really have no idea about the details, plus I didn't want anyone to question why I was nosing around in Paul's background, especially as he's not travelling now. However, what I could see from his files was that there was a police inquiry raised, which suggests some sort of liability. There were no details, I'd have to bother the underwriters if I wanted to find out more. Sorry, but what it does suggest is that Paul has some sort of previous. He's clearly been up to no good but at this moment I have no idea what that no good is. And in my book, that makes him unpredictable and possibly dangerous. I don't want to scare you further, Ella, but I'd be careful if I were you."

Ella digested the information Michelle had given her and began to question her movements over the past few months. "What has he been up to, why has he been stalking me, scaring me, what is he up to..." Ella wondered.

"Why don't you ask Ray to help you? He does work for the police, doesn't he? I'm sure he could pull in a few favours down at his place of work," Michelle reasoned.

"It's not as simple as that. One, he's not an officer so they'd probably close ranks if he asks too many questions, and two, he's Ray's best friend and who do you think he'd believe: me or Paul? I know what you are thinking, Michelle, that he should believe me, but to be honest with you, I'm not sure anymore: after all, I thought you two were having an affair. I got that spectacularly wrong; didn't I. Suppose I involve Ray and he turns against me? I think that is what Paul wants – me out of the way. There needs to be a lot of trust between me and Ray in the first place if he is to believe me ahead of Paul. I know that there is trust between us, well, I think there is, but you know when you're not sure about that one per cent that settles in your mind and won't budge, like an earworm... I'm not sure I want to take that risk with Ray, so I will have to find out what Paul is up to myself. With your help, of course," Ella directed her mock plea at Michelle. "Of course," she replied without hesitation. "I'm sure that if it were me, you'd do the same thing, wouldn't you?"

The first job for the newly convened team of amateur sleuths was to get more information on why there was a question mark on Paul's insurance file. Michelle knew that she had to come up with a watertight excuse that would convince the gatekeepers of privileged information that she absolutely must have the file on Paul Robinson.

Paul had spent a long time determined to learn all he could about Ella. Paul's inquisitive mind had led him to an interest in software for his music, especially word-based software that could enhance his song-writing skills. He was often teased by his peers that he was cheating, and all the most searing and significant song lyrics came from bitter experience, not from a piece of computer code. It did not bother Paul, though, convincing himself that writing song lyrics by using a computer was no different from portrait painters who captured their subjects on photographs before transferring the image to canvas. Paul also knew that he could use software, too, for many of his other activities and interests, legitimate and otherwise. He spent hours learning to code and eventually acquired the skill of creating apps. It was an area of technology that fascinated Paul, to the point where the mysteries of digital creation were, in his mind, no different from putting together chords and words so that they work in perfect harmony.

Ella instinctively knew that Paul's appearance at her office was not an accident. What she could not understand, though, was how he knew her movements, where she would be from one day to the next. It was clear that he knew what time she would be at her desk and wondered what else he knew about her. "Did he know what time I left for work and when I returned, what time I went to lunch," She wondered, not daring to admit to the possibility that Paul did, in fact, know her every move from the moment she left her flat in the mornings to the time she returned home. Even when she visited Ray or when the couple had arranged to go out together. It had indeed been a difficult few days for Ella. However, given what had been happening, she suspected that the days ahead would turn darker and even stranger.

Ella and Ray enjoyed spending hours walking leisurely around London's many markets. It was summer and they felt that they would take advantage of the long evenings and while Greenwich market was a local favourite, and one that they frequently explored, they also liked to venture further into the City whenever they could. It was the end of the working week and Ray smiled when he received a text from Ella suggesting that they meet after work at Spitalfields Market in the busy vicinity of Liverpool Street station. He did not need convincing. The case he was working on – to photograph what was left of a three-car pile-up that was caused by a stolen vehicle - would still be there on Monday morning, he decided. He had filed the photographs carefully, logged the incident, making sure each mangled metal wreck was digitally documented for fingerprints. "Yes, of course. What time and where?"

"I'll meet you at our favourite café in the old part of Spitalfields at 6:30pm," came the reply. Ray spent the rest of the afternoon slightly distracted with excitement, watching the clock until it was time to head to Spitalfields - and therefore, to Ella.

When Ray arrived Ella was waiting, coffee in hand, but she was talking animatedly to Paul. Ray was confused. He could not understand why his friend was talking to his girlfriend. "Hi guys," he said, bending to kiss Ella on the cheek. Hi Paul, I wasn't expecting you to be here too," Ray said. "Yeah, you did, don't you remember telling me that you guys were hanging out here this Friday and you told me to join you?" Ray searched his memory trying to recall the conversation that his friend was referring to. Not wanting to cause a scene or embarrassment, he said, "No I don't, but, well, you're here now, aren't you?"

Ella, though, could barely contain her distress and annoyance at Paul's unexpected appearance, wishing that he was anywhere but here. She knew that he was lying because she'd only made the arrangements with Ray a few hours prior to their meeting, and she also knew that

Ray would not have invited his friend. "He is stalking me, but why," Ella thought to herself while at the same time trying not to let her distress show on her face. She was determined that she would not let the unexpected turn of events ruin the evening that she had carefully arranged with Ray. She did not plan as part of her evening for anyone else to be present. "Did I speak openly in his presence," she wondered. She thought for a while but could not recall any occasion that would provide an answer to her own question.

Ray noticed the upset on his girlfriend's face and uncharacteristically took control. "Paul, hope you don't take this how it sounds, it's not meant to be a brush-off, but I need to speak privately with Ella, so I'm going to ask you to skedaddle, old friend." Ray's familiar good-humoured delivery was enough for Paul to get the message and he bid the lovers farewell. But Paul departed knowing that he had left an indelible imprint on Ella's troubled mind.

"What the hell was that all about," blurted Ella as soon as Paul was out of earshot. "How did he know I was here; did you say anything to him? Did you talk to him after our text?" asked Ella, her understandable anger beginning to rise. Ray calmed her growing anxiety and confirmed that he had not had a conversation with Paul and was equally as surprised as Ella was to see him sitting there when he arrived. "I'll speak to him, don't worry," Ray said. "You'd better speak to him," Ella replied.

The next day Ray got up before his girlfriend, determined to put her at ease and put the events of the previous evening behind her. He prepared breakfast of scrambled eggs and avocado on brown multi-grain toast, washed down with fresh coffee, black, no milk or sugar. "I'm going to speak to Paul this morning, I'll give him a call in a while," he informed Ella. "Well, do it after I've left, please," she said, not wishing to be the unwilling victim of any more of Paul's lies and Ray making excuses for his friend.

The couple spent the next hour and a half enjoying the early morning light that was coming through the open curtains and flooding Ray's bedroom with a freshness that lifted the mood and warmed the atmosphere. More time had passed than either of them had realised. While Ray tried to persuade Ella to stay for a little "hot chocolate" – his not-so-subtle request for mid-morning, post-breakfast sex - Ella had her eye on the fluorescent blue numbers of the digital bedroom clock rather than Ray's obvious intentions. She rebuffed her lover's advances, climbed into the shower, dressed in fitted jeans and a loose top and kissed Ray goodbye. She had arranged to see her mother, always a cue for an engaging day ahead. She dares not be late.

Ray reached for his phone and pressed Paul's number and waited. After four bars of The Who's *Won't Get Fooled Again*, a familiar voice interrupted Roger Daltrey's. "Yo! Ray, what's happening man," Paul answered. "Well, I was hoping you'd tell me," said Ray. "I don't recall telling you that Ella and I were meeting in Spitalfields on Friday, and if I am to be frank with you Paul, Ella was spooked when she saw you. She also said that you bumped into her at the supermarket the other day – you don't even live in

Brockley, Paul. I don't want to know your business; you might have a mate in the area, but Ella said you'd insisted on walking her home, which she declined because she didn't want you to know where she lives."

"Look, Ray, it didn't go down like that, no she's got it wrong, man. I was only being a gentleman, just wanting to help her with the shopping; bags are heavy, you know."

"Paul, we've known each other for years and you've never been that interested in who I date. Now that I've met someone who I am serious about, you seem to take exception to her. What's going on Paul? There's other stuff, too, that Ella told me, such as when you turned up at her workplace, and one evening when you called her asking for me. I didn't even realise that you knew her number, Paul."

"That's not true. She's making stuff up Ray. Who are you gonna believe? Her or me? We've known each other, like, forever, right? Would I lie to you... it's obvious she's losing it, can't trust herself, she doesn't know whether she's coming or going. Look Ray, you'd better get a grip of the situation, man. It seems your girl is letting go of reality. She's crazy, man. I didn't do any of that stuff that she's claiming. Next, she'll be accusing me of all kinds of rubbish that I have no responsibility for. Ray, you believe me, right? I wouldn't lie to you, would I?"

Ray did not respond to his friend's rebuttals and denials and swiftly concluded the conversation on the pretence that he had to answer the door to a delivery driver. Ray had heard enough from Paul and had become unsettled by the fact that he did not recognise this unfamiliar side of his friend. Paul had become agitated and argumentative, talking incessantly as Ray listened, wondering why Paul was acting as if he was trying to talk his way out of a difficult situation while not acknowledging that he may have been doing something that could cause distress to his girlfriend. Paul's response was enough to put Ray on guard. Ella was hoping that her boyfriend would not allow himself to be swayed by Paul's lies. She could think of nothing else while negotiating the traffic to make the short trip to her mother's house. She was aware, too, that her mother would notice immediately if she displayed any hint of emotional distress, so she practised her best poker face, knowing that her mother would pick up on the slightest mood shift in her daughter. "Hi Mum," Ella said, greeting her mother with a wide grin and a hug. Her mother kissed her daughter on each cheek before asking her what was bothering her. "Nothing, honest. I'm fine," Ella bluffed.

"You're not," was her mother's riposte. Ella knew that she did not have anywhere to hide and would have to have a difficult conversation about her personal life with her mum, which was the last thing that she wanted to do, but it was something that she knew that she had to do. She relented.

"Mum, some weird stuff has been happening to me. And before you go off on one of your I-told-you-so sermons, it's not as bad as it sounds, it's just that one of Ray's friends, Paul, the musician pal of his who was at university with Ray, is harassing me. I know it sounds silly and is probably nothing but it could be something. Whatever it is, something is going on, but I don't know what I have done to him, nothing makes sense anymore. I feel powerless. He crops up in my life at the strangest of times and he lies. He lies to me, he lies to Ray, he makes it look as if I am making things up, but I know that I'm not. It's as if he's testing my sanity, or he wants to come between Ray and me, for some reason that I cannot figure out."

Ella's mother listened without saying a word to her daughter. When she was ready to give her opinion, it was not what Ella had expected given their previous discussion about Ray. "It's not you he dislikes, love, he probably has pretty low self-esteem. His behaviour is typical of someone who is less than confident in their own social group. He is probably jealous of you and Ray, and he therefore internalises his inadequacies and the only way he knows how to reassert himself and to re-establish his own boundaries and to make sure that he is important to his friend is to intimidate people who are close to him. This poor chap probably hates himself, I'm sure if you dig deeper, you'd find he's struggling with his own closet of demons. He just wants to be listened to but doesn't know how, so he elects to be nasty to everyone, and it is those who are closest to him who he will lash out at. Did you say he was Ray's best friend?"

"Yes, they are besties – best friends. They studied at the same uni and they're very close, so close in fact, it is unusual to find two men who are so comfortable in each other's company without, well, you know." Ella was grateful and happy that she did not have to listen to one of her mother's lectures on the ills and pitfalls of mixed-race relationships. Grateful, too, that she did not have to argue against her mother's conviction about the unsuitability of black men as spouses and how Paul's behaviour towards her proves her point.

"Mum, I have been feeling really anxious about the situation. I have been imagining things and I have had to second and third guess my every move, I have been asphyxiated by uncertainty because I have become scared that I am not in the right frame of mind to make the right decisions. Even at work I have begun to doubt myself – everyday tasks that I usually do with my eyes shut I am having to check and double check in case I mess up. I have butterflies in my stomach nearly every day - and I am constantly imagining that someone is following me. And I don't even trust myself to share with Ray what I am feeling in case he too thinks that I am losing my mind, in case he doesn't believe me, and I am worried about the impact on our relationship."

Double Double Toil And Trouble

uoyed by the encouraging support from her mother, Ella planned to galvanise those close to her in a determined push to find answers. She included Michelle in her proposed protective cloak of female strength and arranged to meet with her old school pal and new-found gym buddy. She would also call on Rebecca. She needed a reliable support network around her. The three women would get to the bottom of the problem that was Paul.

"Hi Michelle, so what's the plan? Did you get any more information on Paul, what he had been up to at university, you know, the undisclosed bits on his insurance file? I'm eager to know what you've found out. Hopefully it will give us some answers."

"Slow down Ella. No, I don't have any information, I haven't got the answer that you are looking for. These things take time and a clever strategy, but don't worry, I'll get the info. I have a plan; you'll just have to trust me. What about you? What have you been up to, and more importantly, how do you feel? Have you talked over everything with Ray, like I told you to? I'm sure he'll understand; from what I can gather about his character, he'll stand by you. He loves you, Ella, and he won't want to let you down."

"Thanks for your words of encouragement, Michelle. I've bent your ear enough about my problems, but I do have one more favour to ask. I want to be able to feel free again without the sceptre of Paul crippling me with fear. I have Mum, and my sister, Rebecca, and I'd like to feel I can rely on you too because I really don't know why Paul has this view of me and why he is being so apparently vindictive, and I really want to know why. I also don't want to compromise Ray. They are best friends, after all."

"I understand Ella, but Ray must make a choice between you and Paul. If Paul is behaving badly because he doesn't like you – for reasons yet to be established, and probably known only to him – then you must include Ray, not make him choose, but to make him understand that there are boundaries in friendships, and you as his girlfriend, is his priority. And besides, Paul is behaving abominably by going after you."

The women finished their lunchtime conversation and made their way back to their respective place of work. Ella felt reassured that she could rely on Michelle, her secret recruit to her happy band of female musketeers. "We'll emasculate him, Michelle," Ella said.

"Not literally, I hope, though it's not a bad idea," she laughed.

While Michelle was happy to help Ella, she was aware of the demands of her latest essay on social dialects in the English language – due "yesterday". After work, rather than heading home, Michelle made a beeline for the library. Thumbing through the university library's well-stocked collection of books, she found what she was looking for: a discourse on society's elite, the established middle class, the technical middle class, the newly affluent, the emerging classes and why each class bracket has a different way of using the English language. "I know someone who can help me with this," Michelle thought.

The next evening, she knocked on Ray's door in the hope that he would be home. She was in luck. "Please come in. I'll put the coffee on, make yourself at home," said Ray, this time not offering any resistance to Michelle's regular intrusions.

She was pleased that he was home and cheered by the prospect of breaking the back of her essay with Ray's help. "Hi Ray. I've got a few questions for you… yes, coffee please. Black, remember, no milk or sugar," she said.

"Someone who takes their coffee the same way I do," a female voice emerging from the bedroom stated. "This is a pleasant surprise Ella, good to see you, and sorry to barge in, I hope you don't mind but I'm going to borrow your boyfriend for a bit."

"What is it now Michelle? What vexed conundrum would you like me to help you solve today?" Ray said, his voice filled with mocking indignation.

"Well," started Michelle, "I must submit an essay on dialects and want your input. According to conventional wisdom, the social structure of England is made up of different classes, each with its own informal and formal classification and sub-groups and within these different classes and sub-groups, the dialect is used to determine where you're from and if you fit into a certain sub-group, even the names we use is a determinant, something that places the individual in a particular social box that they rarely move out of. I think with globalisation, that strict linguistic constraint rooted in demography and place has been broken down, which is where you come in Ray. In Jamaica, what do you call your evening meal?" asked Michelle.

"Dinner," came Ray's reply. "Tea," chimed Ella. "See what I mean, immediately, both of you have been placed in different categories. When is a napkin a serviette? Or, picking up on your contribution, Ella, dinner can also become supper, or pudding, and in some households, it is called dessert."

"We always have dessert at home," Ella said. "While he's not my favourite person, Paul is a good example of what I think you are talking about, Michelle. He often speaks in a streetwise, chummy sort of way when he's out with his mates, but I've heard him sound like a college professor when he's being serious. It's very selective, if a bit weird, if you ask me, but he uses language like a key to get in and out of certain social circles. Would you agree, Ray," she said, turning to the person who knows him best. "S'pose so," responded Ray.

The conversation around language and class continued, each person finding funnier and more peculiar terms that are used interchangeably by different classes. By the end of the evening, Michelle felt that she had enough to complete her essay and Ella knew that Michelle was not a threat. "Michelle, I'm going to the gym next week. I have a Pilates session starting at 7:30 in the evening, will you be there?"

"Yes, I will, but I won't be doing Pilates, I will, though, be pushing some weights – I have a circuit that I do to make sure I can get into my clothes, which is an ongoing problem these days, especially as I like cakes and the odd glass of wine." Both women laughed. "You can meet Rebecca, too. You'll like her," Ella said.

"Hello! There's someone else here... this is my flat, my space. I am feeling ostracised and neglected," Ray called out.

"Can you hear something in the background Michelle?"

"No, I can't, can you?"

"Didn't think so... Now, where were we...." The two women laughed at Ray's expense.

The following Thursday, as arranged, Michelle met Ella at the gym, where she introduced Michelle to Rebecca. "Pleased to meet you. I've heard a lot about you, and of course, have seen you here in the gym looking all impressive and stuff as you push those weights around," Rebecca said. "Likewise, pleased to meet you too," replied Michelle. "Although we have met before, many, many years ago. I understand that you've been very supportive of Ella. She really needs it right now, I'm sure you know what I am talking about. We must get this weirdo off her back, right? How was the class?"

It was clear that Simona, the Pilates teacher, had put her students through their paces. Both Ella and Rebecca were glistening from all the effort of pulling and pushing and stretching and panting of the past 45-minutes.

"There's a coffee shop no more than two minutes away from the gym, shall we convene for a quick dose of caffeine and a chat?" Ella did not get any objections from the other women.

"Did you get any more info on Paul, Michelle? I have filled Rebecca in on the fact that you might have some information on his previous misdemeanours."

"Yes, and no. I have been digging, but as I said, getting hold of the file is not that easy, but I have been using our innate advantage, the one thing a man can't use to get the upper hand, and it's the one thing that they fall victim to: our femininity. There's a new broker at work who fancies himself as a bit of a ladies' man, a player, so we had a few drinks the other day and I made up an excuse as to why I need to see Paul's file, I fed him a yarn about a discrepancy on Paul's form and something about him never completing his forms properly. The eager young pup seems to have bought the yarn I spun him. I promised to have a drink with him after work, so I should get the info soon," she laughed, congratulating herself on her wily manoeuvre.

"Well done, Michelle. I can't wait, hopefully it will give me some idea why Paul appears to be so against me dating Ray."

"And it will stop you coming over like an emotional shipwreck, too," added Rebecca. "I'm not used to seeing you like this. It'll be like old times to see you not in a constant state of anxiety because of your boyfriend's best mate," she added with an intended heavy delivery of contempt.

When the time came for Michelle to play her role, she looked up from her desk to see a smiling Damian looking down at her while waving a thick file. "I have what you want," he said with a lascivious smile. "But you can only have it if you keep your promise to have a drink with me," he said, continuing to wave the file in front of Michelle that contained all the information she needed on Paul Robinson.

"Sure Damian, I'm a woman of my word, but I'm an expensive date, but first let me see the file to check that I didn't enter the incorrect details relating to Mr Robinson's last trip because as I'm sure you are aware, we aren't allowed to take personal files out of the office, right?"

"Yes, of course, here you are." Michelle knew that she only had a few minutes to scrutinise the file in the pretence that she was checking her own work. She scanned the reams of paper quickly, while all the time being extremely careful not to arouse the suspicions of her colleague as to her true intent, relying on the fact that he was too distracted by the thought of spending an evening with Michelle. What she saw among the bundle of papers startled her.

"Thanks Damien, here's the file, everything is in order after all, but at least I can stop worrying now. As I am a woman of my word, I'll see you in the bar after work. Don't be late, will you? I don't like to be kept waiting for what I want." She flashed Damian a warm, friendly flirtatious smile, waited till he had returned to his own office before making meticulous notes of the details of what she had seen on Paul Robinson's file.

She reached for her phone and dialled. "Hi Ella, meet me tomorrow after work in Greenwich at our usual coffee shop. I'll be there at 6:30 sharp. I have some news for you."

The news that Michelle had for Ella would either make her feel better or increase her anxiety tenfold, thought Michelle. She was concerned but realised that her friend had to be told the truth. She deserves to know why Paul was behaving the way he had been towards her.

"Ella, this is shocking, so brace yourself. I had to scribble down the info from the file, which I only had in my possession for a few minutes while my colleague stood over me. Fortunately, on this occasion he was more interested in ogling me than being concerned about what I was really up to. And you really don't want to hear what I had to go through to get this piece of information. Anyway, while Paul was in his first year of university, he had three cautions against him for stalking a fellow first-year student. It was on the third occasion when the police were called, and the student was so traumatised by the experience that she left university and transferred to another undergraduate course at another institution, the name of which was classified. The classified information on his file is simply because the police had become involved. Here's where it gets weird and worrying: her name is Ellie Sackville-Hayes, she is tall with an athletic build and long, thick, tumbling auburn hair. Who does that remind you of Ella?" Ella was lost for words, visibly shocked by what she'd heard. The description and the name were too close to her own for comfort, even the double-barrelled denotation, but the information was welcome, if a little disturbing bordering on the traumatic, as it gave Ella a possible understanding of why Paul was being so aggressively predatory.

"Ella, Ella... are you still with me? Have another glug of coffee. Mmm, it looks like you might possibly need something stronger because there's more information. After a while, Paul would turn up at her digs unannounced and would follow her around at all sorts of times of day, even hanging around outside her halls of residence at night. According to the notes on the file, they shared a brief relationship that seemed to end as abruptly as it started. My take on it, and I am only speculating here, is that I think his advances were rejected, and presumably he didn't take the rejection well and as is often the case with these situations, he took the rejection from Ellie as an insult to his male ego. I've read about his stuff and often the stalker targets someone above their own social class, and by declaring their love for that person, they see it was a way of elevating their own perceived status."

"Thanks for the insight, Michelle, but I think Paul is delusional and probably mentally ill. I must talk to Ray about it. Ray needs to know that his best friend is not what he seems and is probably quite dangerous."

Ella reached for her phone and attempted to call Ray but given the state of shock that she was in, she could not recall his number, a number she knew as assuredly as she knew her own birthday. Michelle, registering her friend's distress, offered to call Ray. She took Ella's phone and began to type Ray's number, considering it a stroke of luck that she had previously exchanged numbers with Ray. It was then that Michelle noticed a strange message flash up on the screen. It was enough to alert her, and to provide answers to a lot of Ella's unanswered questions. An aspect of Michelle's work in insurance meant that she was aware of many of the possible scams that fraudsters used to extract and launder money. The notification flashed up and disappeared just as quickly, but it was visible long enough to make Michelle gasp in surprise. Her due diligence training meant that she immediately knew what it was, and more importantly, she knew how to retrieve the message from the darker reaches of a smartphone.

"Update on Ellie is ready to view."

"Ella, I think you need to see this message," said Michelle.

"What!" exclaimed Ella, hardly believing what her eyes were reading. She returned her phone to Michelle, not trusting herself not to throw it out into the busy Greenwich streets. She felt an immediate chill course through her. Ella gasped for breath. She felt as if the walls of the café were closing in on her; she felt sick. She attempted to move but felt her knees become unstable as if her legs would let her down. Michelle looked on in concern for her friend. "It's stalkerware," she informed Ella. "You'd better not attempt to stand up. You probably won't make it to your feet."

Her friend's words were like a light illuminating her darkness. Suddenly everything that had been happening to Ella in the past few months made sense. She wasn't going mad. She wasn't losing her mind. And with the information that Michelle had found on Paul's insurance file, everything began to make sense.

"Someone's been using a surveillance program to track your every move," Michelle confirmed. "Someone's been reading all your messages, seeing your screen activity, where you go and when, using GPS locations... Girl, you've been played by someone who has got it in for you. And I don't think it's an accident that the name that flashed up was Ellie, not Ella," was Michelle's summation of the situation. "Is Paul the culprit," she asked. Deep down, Ella knew exactly who had been turning her world upside down. But what she really wanted to know was why Paul had conflated her with the woman whom he had met at university and whose life he had turned into a living nightmare to such an extent that she had to leave her university course. She called Ray to tell him what she knew.

"It's clear that he has some serious, deep psychological issues and he hasn't learnt anything from his past brush with authority," said Michelle. "How was he able to install the stalkerware program on your phone, Ella? It can only be done if the person physically has your phone." Ella thought back to all the possible occasions when Paul would have had the opportunity. Was it at Ray's flat, she wondered? "The only time I can remember him having access to my phone was after his trip to Moscow earlier in the year when he borrowed it to call his mum on his return to the UK. I had no idea what he was up to. I had no reason not to trust his intentions. I should have asked myself at the time why he didn't ask to use Ray's phone, but I was driving. It all makes sense now. I feel like a gullible chump," Ella said.

"How would you have known? Don't beat yourself up about it, Ella, he's at fault here, not you," Michelle reassured. "What you need is a holiday. I'm taking a short break to Spain next week, why don't you come with me? You'd love it, and it will be the perfect antidote to all the nonsense that you've had to put up with from Paul over the summer. Accommodation is sorted as I have a friend that I stay with, so all you need to do is concern yourself with your flight and spending money. Deal?" Ella did not need to give Michelle's proposal a second thought. First, she had to finish her conversation with Ray about his best friend.

Ella and Michelle departed, Ella making her way to Ray's flat while Michelle made her way home. When she arrived, Ray was eager to find out exactly what the amateur sleuths had dug up. Ella shared what she had learnt from Michelle and asked Ray if he was aware of what had taken place at university. "No, I had no idea. Paul's a great guy but he does keep his cards close to his chest at times, even from me. He's so into his music I just put down any odd behaviour as the idiosyncrasies of the artistic mind, you know how these artists can be a bit intense," Ray said.

"He's not a great guy, Ray. He's a misogynist and has some deep psychological issues around self-worth. He needs help, Ray, and if you are a true friend, you should talk to him, let him know in no uncertain terms what he has put me through these past few months, how he has affected my mental health out of some warped sense of revenge because I just happen to look like an unattainable woman he had a thing for at university, despite the fact that that woman said no - for a reason. He needs to know, too, what the effects of his actions had on Ellie. We don't even know how she is now. She may still be living in fear because of Paul. She might find it difficult to start, let alone maintain, a loving relationship because of what Paul did, whatever he did. What gives him the right to pursue and persecute her just because she wasn't interested in his advances? Is there anything else that we don't know about Paul and what he might have done to this poor girl?"

"You're right Ella. I know this has been awful for you and I am sorry that I probably haven't been there for you because of work, but I had no idea what Paul was up to, and I can't get my head around the fact that he somehow sees you as this other woman. That's seriously disturbed. Don't worry, I'll take care of it. I'll make sure he won't bother you again – or anyone else for that matter. I'll speak with your dad. I'm sure Stephen will have something to say about his behaviour towards you. Your dad probably knows people in the criminal justice system who could shed some light on Paul, if in fact he does have some previous."

"No, leave Dad out of this. He does know people, but they are the sort of people whose company he shouldn't be keeping given that he is a successful criminal barrister. Err, one more thing Ray, I'm taking a short break to Spain with Michelle. She invited me to go with her and there's no reason I can think of not to. We leave at the weekend. I need a break. I'll call you when I get back."

Girl Power

It had been a difficult few weeks for Ella. She had been left emotionally exhausted by Paul's relentless attempts to come between her and Ray and to undermine her, so when Michelle invited her to spend a few days in Oviedo, she did not need a second more than was necessary before accepting. When Michelle called to confirm the details, Ella said: "My bags are packed," she giggled excitedly at the prospect of getting away from the psychological trauma that she had been subjected to, a period that had stretched her relationship with Ray to breaking point, had made her question their relationship and had almost caused her to fall out with her mother. She felt, too, that her boyfriend had not done enough to protect her from his best friend. She was hoping that a few days away will give Ray some time to think about their relationship, for him to think about why he should give her more of his time.

The mid-morning flight from London Heathrow touched down in Oviedo in the late afternoon. The flight had been uneventful, with only the short interlude in Madrid to break up the journey. During the flight the two women chatted animatedly, Michelle spending most of the flight reassuring Ella that everything will be fine and that she should demand that Ray cut all ties with Paul because of his unreason able behaviour and the fact that given the circumstances, Ella is potentially in danger of whatever he is capable of, particularly as his calculating nastiness was not rooted in normal or reasonable behaviour.

They were met at Ovicdo airport by Frankie. Michelle flung her arms around her friend in unbridled excitement before remembering that she had a guest. "This is Ella, my girlfriend that I told you about who's been having a hard time - to put it mildly. She's looking forward to some good old R&R, I told her she would be in good hands," Michelle said. The weather was still hot and balmy for a mid-August evening in Northern Spain. The Galena winds that caress the Bay of Biscay and swoop over from the Cantabrian Sea had yet to show its brutish side, which was a blessing for Ella as the warm evenings were a much-needed antidote to the dark clouds that had engulfed Ella and lifted her mood.

The day-long journey from London to Oviedo had meant that Ella and Michelle could do little more than collapse into bed after a quick shower, a light Mediterranean snack of anchovies, black olives, juicy red tomatoes and a selection of local cheeses, wine, and a quick catch up with Frankie. The next morning Ella woke up and marvelled at the sparkling light and breathed in the freshness of the air. After breakfast, Michelle and Ella spent the day meandering around the chic boutiques of the city and visited what seemed like every tourist attraction that held even the slightest appeal. Before long the afternoon had turned into early evening and in the fading sun Michelle persuaded Ella that a late lunch and an evening stroll around the medieval old town and Oviedo's striking Gothic cathedral, where she promised that the fading embers of the golden sunlight would lift her spirits and help her to put behind her Paul's horrific and malicious scheming of the past few months.

"Thanks for being there for me, Michelle," Ella said, not knowing how her appreciation would be greeted. Their relationship had got off to an uncertain start, and if Michelle had not wanted anything to do with her, Ella would have understood. But she knew that she had Michelle to thank for discovering the spyware on her phone – planted there, she now knows – by Paul. She was appreciative, too, that Michelle laughed off the fact that Ella thought she was the "other woman", even though there was no "other woman" intent on breaking up her relationship with Ray. Even now she felt embarrassed at the thought that she initially saw the woman she was walking through a Spanish plaza with as her enemy.

"How are you feeling now," Michelle asked Ella, fully aware of the fragility of her friend's state of mind. "You've been dragged through the emotional mill by that bastard, Paul, and all because he seems to have some warped, misguided issues about you somehow being someone who just happens to look like you and have a similar-sounding name. It's a fucked-up idea that is obviously being driven by him being rejected by her; he probably hates you too for dating his best friend."

"No, I think it is more complicated than that, Michelle. When Ray and I spoke about him, Ray said he was unaware of Paul's darker side, but did say he does at times have some random and disconnected thoughts, usually about some song lyric he's unpicked, that he then obsesses over, seeing meaning where there is none, but Ray said he usually ignores him. He comes across as Mr Metropolitan, but I always found it strange that he would read a lot of the more militant literature that was around during the troubling period of 60s America, he has some strange ideas, too, about race relations and he believes that Ray and I shouldn't be together because he's black and I'm white, yet the girl at uni was white. None of it makes sense. It's all crap, but what can I do about it? I had enough stick from my mum about me and Ray being together; I didn't expect it and didn't need it from my boyfriend's supposed best friend."

"He's a nasty piece of work, let's change the subject," interrupted Michelle. "But first, and from the perspective of a black woman, you must realise that not everyone is happy about mixed-race relationships, Ella. Black men feel they must live up to a stereotypical nightmare scenario of every white male throughout history of having their women seduced and defiled by a well-hung black man. Ray and I have had conversations about this. I called it the Mandingo Theory. Ray, of course, had no idea what I was talking about, bless him. Black men also have massive hang-ups about black women dating white men, and some black women feel betrayed by black men dating white women. The whole thing is a nuanced, multi-layered mess, really, and there aren't any real answers. I like to think that when I fall in love, it is with the person and not the stereotype of what that person is supposed to be in the eyes of society at large."

Ella listened, thoughts of her own relationship running through her head. "What does that say about multiculturalism? Is it dead, an idealistic idyll that is ultimately unobtainable, and what does it say about the feminist movement that ignores black women?" said Ella. "That, my girl, is another conversation," Michelle laughed as they strolled through the square, walking hand in hand, weaving in and out of the locals enjoying the balmy evening and taking in the evening ambience of the diners eating their late supper washed down by jugs of sangria.

"Michelle, can I ask why you always wear black, it suits you, of course, but I don't think I have ever seen you in any other colour. Is it a subliminal statement?" she asked. "No, nothing so erudite or meaningful, I'm afraid. I wear black because I like black. And as you say, it suits me, and it suits my skin colour. Black skin comes in many, many different shades, Ella, and my autumn-brown tone contrasts perfectly with black. I like it. It's me. It's my style, my signature. Now, can I ask you a question. Would you mind if I continue to steal your man from time to time – purely for academic reasons, you understand."

"No, of course not. As long as he doesn't get the wrong impression of your minx-like sassiness and make a fool of himself. If that happens, promise me you'll be gentle with him." The two women laughed at the image of Ray struggling to make sense of Michelle's openly sexual demeanour. "What do you think of Frankie," asked Michelle seeking approval. "The flat is small but I'm sure you'll have a great stay. As a host, Frankie is so easy-going that you should just make yourself at home and not worry about a thing," she added, her hands now folded comfortably into Ella's as they strolled back to the flat where they were greeted by Frankie's outstretched arms, each hand holding a glass of wine – one for Ella, one for Michelle. They settled down and the conversation flowed. Michelle, with Ella's blessing, relayed her friend's trauma to Frankie, who looked on in shock and growing anger. Before long, three empty bottles were laid out on the teak table that held centre stage in the sitting room, Miles Davis blew his trumpet in the background and as Ella gazed out of the window looking beyond the town towards the peaks of the Parque Nacional de Los Picos de Europa in the far distance, she did indeed feel relaxed.

She felt relaxed and was so enchanted by the ambience of Northern Spain's centuries-old city that she did not notice that Michelle and Frankie had disappeared into the bedroom. The evening heat mixed with the wine was intoxicating. Ella threw back her head, allowing her wavy hair to fall unkempt down her bare back. The warm evening breeze played with her senses, so much so that she did not notice that Michelle had come back into the sitting room, dressed this time in nothing more than a flowing robe, open at the front revealing her black lacy underwear. "Are you ok," she asked. "Yes, I'm loving the atmosphere. It's hot though, but the breeze is so soothing, thanks."

"You express your gratitude too often. It really is no problem, I'm happy to help," Michelle said. Ella watched Michelle glide over to the extravagantly stocked fridge, yanking the heavy door open so that her robe, too, parted to reveal a curvaceous figure that flattered and enchanted. Squatting to reach down for a bottle of water, Ella could not help but notice Michelle's firm thighs and rounded buttocks as she stood and walked back into the bedroom, allowing her robe to fall to the floor as she reached the bedroom door to reveal a perfectly tapered back that dovetailed into her peachy posterior. Ella stared at Michelle, sipped her wine, licked her lips, reaching up with her free hand to unconsciously caress her breast, at no time taking her eyes off Michelle's body as she returned to Frankie's soft caresses. "My God!" Ella exclaimed to herself, shocked at the idea that she might be turned on by Michelle. She let out a laugh that was barely audible and put her wandering thoughts of Michelle down to the wine and the seductive night air.

This was not the first time, though, that she had admired Michelle's physique, there were many occasions in the gym that she had looked admiringly at her toned, perfectly proportioned body as she moved from one weight machine to another, each time bossing the heavy slabs of metal into submission. Her too-long glances were then no more than an idle wonder where she had seen her before. Now though, her attraction to Michelle was more than an aesthetic appreciation, it was more of a visceral reaction to her undeniable beauty. Ella peered towards the open bedroom door and was able to make out Michelle's strong legs being kissed by Frankie, her lover's long black hair falling and lifting over Michelle's honey-hued lower back, each millimetre being kissed softly, moving towards her thighs, Frankie's sun-drenched olive skin blending perfectly with the autumn brown of Michelle's tone that contrasted so perfectly with her predictable black attire. Ella looked on; her silhouette framed by the open window as she bathed in the evening heat that wafted its way into Frankie's small flat. She felt a bead of sweat roll down her chest and come to a salty halt briefly before continuing its journey down her exposed décolletage. She instinctively raised her hand and wiped away the sweat, subconsciously moving her fingers softly over her breasts, her nipple responding to her touch. At that moment Michelle returned to the fridge for ice. She noticed that Ella's eyes were fixed on her. Michelle turned around to face Ella, her robe tantalisingly revealing much more than it did before, and Ella's stomach responded with an ache that she only felt when she was aroused. "Do you like what you see, Ella? I notice that you have been staring at me appreciatively for a while now. It's quite flattering, and I don't mind at all; you're a bit of a catch yourself, too, you know. At least you now know that I am in a same-sex relationship. Yes,

Francesca and I are partners. We can't always choose who we love. On the contrary, love chooses us. Besides, I believe that we are all born with the ability to be attracted to both men and women, regardless of our gender. I simply do not allow convention or society to determine who I love and who I sleep with." After a long pause between the two women, their eyes momentarily fixed on each other, Michelle said, "Would you like to join us in the bedroom? I can sense that you are turned on, besides, you shouldn't deny your feelings, and Frankie is a very considerate and accommodating lover." Ella paused, hesitated, and held back her response to Michelle.

"Mmm! Ella, look. There is a chasm between how a woman sees herself, I mean truly sees herself, and how the rest of society sees her. A woman's body has been commodified, owned, commented on, ogled at and taken advantage of by men. The result is a woman's pleasure has been suppressed and distorted. We are barely able to recognise ourselves anymore. The ownership of our sexuality has been yanked from our grasp by the male gaze purely for their pleasure, while our pleasure is left to rot and fester. This has been going on for centuries. And what about our sexual and intellectual pleasure? Why can't we as women be sexy and clever at the same time? Ella, you are denying your feelings because of society's entrenched rules about what it is to be a woman, a woman who can express herself sexually without having to subjugate her intellect too. You and I both have grown up despising how we look. It's the default mode for so many young women who hate their thighs at the age of 14 and continue unknowingly down the path of self-deprecation over how we view ourselves, our sexuality and our body image. It can be ruinous to one's self-esteem. Personally, I took the decision years ago not to buy into that male narrative. This is me: sexy and smart. I love being who I am because it makes me feel free of the constraints imposed by the unfair hand that too many women are left with. It puts us at an immediate disadvantage in this ongoing game of body politics."

Ella pondered Michelle's invitation to join her and Frankie. Michelle's strident boldness caught Ella off-guard, but it was nonetheless, not unexpected from this enigmatic woman. She always wondered about Michelle's sexuality, which appeared to be at best fluid, and most intriguingly, wrapped in ambiguity. Over the summer months that their relationship had been transformed from potential adversaries to friends, Ella had never seen Michelle with a man, and she now understood what she meant when she said that Ray wasn't her type. Michelle's views left Ella asking herself if Ray was indeed her type. Up till now she had no doubt. However, Michelle challenged her ideas of feminism and what it is to be a woman and how she frames her relationship with Ray. Ella considered herself a feminist, she saw herself as Ray's equal in every aspect of their relationship. However, the stone that Michelle had thrown into the pond had created ripples of self-doubt about her femininity and led to questions that she wasn't prepared to find the answers to.

Ella finished her glass of wine, glanced up at the fading light of the late evening and welcomed the calming breeze as it wafted over her chilled skin. She turned to Michelle and smiled. "This is not the time to unpick my relationship with Ray." Her inner thoughts were whispered quietly and softly enough so that Michelle could not respond.

Helping Hand

Oviedo was just the lift that Ella needed, and she felt eternally grateful for Michelle and Frankie for hosting her, holding her hands, boosting her confidence, feeding, and watering her, with wine mostly, and returning her to a sense of normality, a cheery calmness that she was afraid would not return. The only thing that she had missed was Ray. However, she hoped that he would step up to the plate and ask Paul some tough questions. Ray had promised her that he would, but given his passive nature, she could not be sure he had what it took to follow through on his promise. She knew, though, that she could rely on her ingenuity and guile, and call on the help of Michelle and Rebecca to get to the bottom of why Paul had targeted her as the object of his vilification.

Rebecca was eager to help her sister regain her mojo. She was not about to let Ella slip further down the road of suffering at the hands of a person that she did not know but someone who she was convinced was nothing more than the worst type of social bully. She would do anything she could to achieve some sort of closure for Ella. Rebecca knew that Paul did not know that his harassment of Ella had been found out, which gave Ella and her gang of amateur sleuths an advantage in their quest of exposing Paul. And Rebecca had a plan. The only question that remained was whether Ella was strong and courageous enough to go along with what Rebecca had in mind, after all, it was Ella's mental health and wellbeing on the line, not hers or Michelle's. The plan had been agreed, the terms of engagement had been carefully scripted. All Rebecca was waiting for was the green light from Ella.

Ella was keen to see Ray on her return from Spain and had arranged for him to visit after he had finished work. Ella unpacked her suitcase before going to the supermarket to stock up: milk, bread, fruits, she trawled through the list that she had made on her phone. It was then that she was reminded that it had become normal to submit all aspects of our lives to our phones; our wants, wishes and desires. Our plans, our fears and our ambitions. "Paul will probably know what we'll be eating this evening," she laughed. She vowed that she would take Rebecca's advice and not commit every aspect of her life to her phone. Rebecca had bought her a fountain pen and a small notepad while she was away, leaving them on the kitchen table in plain sight for when Ella returned from Spain. The pen and the notepad were a deliberate metaphorical prod from Rebecca for Ella to get back to basics, to rely on her instincts and not to be so eager and willing to see the good in everyone - even if their intention was less than honest.

It would be a new way of living for Ella. Unlike many of her generation or her sister, she was not a fan of social media: she could not see what led so many of her peers to give in to an insatiable need to share with the world every aspect of their daily lives. Ella used her phone for nothing more exciting than communicating with others through text or a simple call - and for making notes, logging appointments and shopping lists. Her reliance on her phone was as a result of treating her hand-held device like a virtual personal assistant; it would be hard to break that habit: her calendar was her crutch. Every date with the gym, her hairdresser, her mum, meet-ups with girlfriends and more besides would be entered into her phone's calendar and checked before she committed to anything, but she knew that it was important to wrestle away from her assailant the advantage of knowing her every move.

She had grown excited with anticipation of Ray's arrival. The bottle of Rioja on the table was a reminder of her long weekend in Spain and was to be a celebration of her being reunited with Ray. Crab linguine with chilli and parsley – she decided to leave the garlic out of the recipe on this occasion – had been lovingly prepared. Ray wanted to know all about her trip and how she got on with Michelle. She did not spare any detail, recalling the beguiling buildings and the seductive atmosphere. "And what's Frankie like?" Ray inquired. "She's great, a really lovely woman and perfect for Michelle," Ella said. "She? I thought Frankie was a he, not a she. Are you telling me that Michelle's partner is a woman?"

"Yes, I am. Do you have a problem with that Ray?"

Ray did a poor job of hiding his surprise at the news about Michelle. Ray held a preconceived notion that a woman in a same-sex relationship looked and behaved in a certain way, views that were probably influenced by the amount of time that he spent with his colleagues at the Met or his church-going parents whose opinions were chiselled from the strict interpretation of the Bible, which did not leave any room for loving anyone other than the opposite sex. He checked his own prejudices and quietly chided himself for thinking that maybe Michelle was coming on to him, and, embarrassed by the thought, vowed not to be so judgemental in the future.

"And what have you been up to while I was away? I supposed you've been hanging out with Paul, partying, and drinking too much, right?" Ray considered the question before answering. Ray was still trying to make sense of Paul's recent behaviour, why he had harassed the girl at university to such an extent that she had to leave her course, and her new-found friends to complete her degree elsewhere. He thought he knew as much as it was possible to know about Paul, but now he was wondering not what he knew about Paul, but what he didn't know.

He had promised Ella that he would take care of it, and he was determined to keep his word. As far as he was concerned, Paul had overstepped the mark of loyalty, and he had betrayed any trust between them, and his actions towards Ella was unforgivable and more importantly for Ray, Paul's behaviour did not give any consideration to their friendship.

He had seen Paul, but not as often as his girlfriend had assumed. "I met up with Paul once, and then only briefly. We've both been busy over the past few days, not enough time to party." Ella, though, was hoping to hear that he had at least asked Paul to give account of himself as to why he was harassing his girlfriend and at best had reported him to the police. She was not surprised that nothing had been done, she'd become accustomed to Ray's laid-back approach to life – even if the severity of the situation called for more strident, considered action.

Ray knew, though, that by reporting the actions of his friend to the police without hard evidence of something that happened some years ago would not go very far in achieving a conviction, or even getting the attention of the police investigators. His experience of working for the police gave him the insight that there were other ways to take care of Paul. Rebecca, though, shared Ella's expectations of Ray and was equally as unimpressed at the perceived lack of action from Ray. Her remedy for his inaction was to concoct her plan that she would share with Ella and Michelle. First, they had to find out why Paul had terrorised Ellie and why he was now doing the same to Ella. Rebecca had an intuitive feeling that there was more to Paul's actions than just the uncanny set of similarities between the two women.

On her return to London, Ella felt rested and had put any thought of Paul and Ellie behind her, preferring to bask in the memories of the roller-coaster of emotion that was Oviedo. She woke up with a renewed skip in her stride. The four-day break with Michelle had seemed longer than it actually was, and she put that down to the change in the regular routine of commuting and work. She pushed her way on to the DLR, finding a seat at the back of the driverless train where she was able to sit down and lose herself in a book for the 25-minute journey to Canary Wharf. As she alighted, her phone rang. It was Rebecca. "Hi Ella, meet me after work in the pub on Blackheath. Let Michelle know too. I've got a plan."

Over glasses of wine, Rebecca reminded the gathered that harassment was against the law while bullying was offensive behaviour in its simplest form. She then assigned Ella and Michelle to the task of monitoring and documenting every contact or attempted contact Paul had with Ella, while she would scour social media for any trace of Ellie Sackville-Hayes. While she knew that her sister had the scantest footprint on social media, Rebecca, though, lived and breathed social media and felt a surge of excitement at every tweet, every post and every notification that pinged on her phone.

"This won't be easy, Ella," warned Michelle. "It will be distressing and probably disturbing and frightening, but this time you're wise to his antics. And you have us, we've got your back." The three amateur investigators were setting traps they hoped Paul would walk right into. They knew, however, that they had the advantage of knowing that Paul did not know that they knew that he was harassing Ella. The longer they could maintain their advantage over Paul, the more chance they had of ensnaring and exposing him.

Ray, too, was plotting and scheming how to catch Paul out and how this person he now considers a former friend would be dealt with. He thought about pulling in a few favours from officers that he was certain would jump at the chance of going rogue, turning a blind eye, bending the rules to entrap a target. It was not unusual for some members of the force to risk their salary, their pensions, their freedom and their career for a backhander that in some cases amounted to less than a month's wage after tax. Ray also knew that there was always the possibility that the infamous canteen culture that operates like a noticeboard of gossip for officers would run the risk of his name being talked about. If he spoke out of turn to the wrong officer, it would lead to him losing his job, his impeccably unblemished reputation and possibly Ella. It's nothing more than blackmail should he go down that route. No, he'd have to find another, more ingenious way to exact revenge on Ella's behalf. Ray was not a police officer, and he was only too aware of that. His job spec was to serve as a liaison between the actual police officers and the crime lab, a glorified civil servant, a scientist who gathers information. Anything more than that and he knew he would be overreaching his position as an employee of the Metropolitan Police.

Ray found his answer to how to get back at Paul while listening to the radio. The range of options on DAB radio was a source of excitement to Ray, who grew up in an environment where the transistor radio was the conduit for every piece of news that was broadcast across the Caribbean. A leftover habit from his time in Jamaica, Ray enjoyed the clipped tones of the radio presenters playing in the background. Radio held a special part in Ray's upbringing: there was always a radio somewhere while he was growing up in Jamaica, but the little black boxes carrying news, music and gossip commanded centre stage whenever the West Indies cricket team was playing, particularly when the opponents were England. Every boundary struck by the boys against the Mother Country and every wicket that was shattered and scattered about the 22 would be a cue for riotous celebration. The radio brought the action happening at Lord's or Headingly, directly to Sabina Park in Kingston. However, playing in the background on Ray's radio was not a Test between the West Indies and England, but a news piece that caught his attention. The presenters had introduced an item about forensic photography, which jerked Ray's mind back from cricket and his childhood and piqued his interest. He listened to the programme in the hope that he'd learn something about his profession that he didn't already know. But what he did learn planted the seeds of an idea by which he'd get back at Paul. Ray listened entranced as the voice coming from the radio waxed lyrical about how infrared hand variations taken using special infrared cameras highlights oxygenated blood, rendering the blood flowing through the arteries like tramlines, mapping a pattern like a town-planner's grid system, and if the unique patterns, skin colour and marks of the culprit matches a previously captured image, you have your man. Ray realised that the new and exciting technique in forensic science was more suited to intruders or sex offenders, but he could see that he could also use it to corner Paul. His next task was to photograph Paul's hands. He didn't know how he was going to do that until, while on his way to work, he noticed a poster splashed on the side of a passing bus advertising the latest exhibition at the National Portrait Gallery. It gave him the idea of photographing all his friends under the guise of testing out a new forensic technique. That way he would be able to capture Paul's infrared handprint so that if he in any way threatened Ella again, he would have the evidence that he needed to act. The second part of his plan was to erect surveillance cameras at Ella's house in the hope of capturing an infrared image of Paul's hand. And he knew how he would accomplish that.

"Hi Paul, fancy going out tonight, it's Friday and I haven't seen you in a while." Ray had decided to give his university friend a call in the hope that he could entice him out. First, though, he planned to call around to Ella's in the hope that the newly installed infrared cameras would capture Paul's hands in enough detail. "I've got to call round to Ella's so it might be best if you meet me here, we'll head up to Brockley to see Ella, then to the pub. How does that sound?" Paul agreed that the arrangement was indeed sensible. There was no reason for him to question Ray's itinerary. Ray was pleased with himself. He nodded approvingly in a self-congratulatory way in the belief that he had set a watertight trap.

Spot The Difference

Michelle and Rebecca knew that tracking down a former student named Ellie Sackville-Hayes would be difficult, if not impossible. The only lead she had to go on was that Ellie was at university with Paul, which meant that they at least had the correct year. Which university she moved on to was and remained a mystery. But Rebecca was resolute in her determination to find answers to the burning question as to why Paul had fixated on Ella, and the only way to find answers was to speak to Ellie. She knew, too, that her social media skills, her ability to navigate the more mysterious and subterranean corners of Instagram, TikTok and Twitter, would prove useful in tracking down the hard-to-find Ellie Sackville-Hayes.

Rebecca made the calculation that at least six years had passed since the woman who was the focus of her investigation and Paul were at university together. The pair had met at the student bar one evening when getting to know your fellow undergraduate was as important as getting to know which lectures to attend and which ones to skip, which lecherous lecturer to avoid and which would be most useful in the first few weeks of that important first year at university. Paul and Ray were drinking beer with other students in their class when they noticed Ellie and three friends enter the student bar. What they hadn't noticed was that their presence had been noted by Grace, a gregarious member of Ellie's party. Grace did not waste any time dragging her three girlfriends over to where the boys were sitting, much to Ellie's embarrassment and protest. But rather than a wasted night, Ellie had taken a liking to Paul, finding his quirky sense of humour and his obvious intellect appealing, so much so that she was flattered when Paul asked to see her again.

Paul knew that the student bar was not romantic enough and a restaurant was too expensive on a student's budget. He wanted to create a space where he could impress, to talk and get to know Ellie, get to understand her likes and dislikes. He didn't know what she was studying but was determined to find out; he had decided ahead of their meeting that he would present himself as a perfect gent, would listen to her, allow her to explore her feelings, be supportive and make her feel comfortable.

Communication, he thought, was the perfect opening gambit in what he thought could be a promising romance. "I'll be thoughtful, considerate and just be myself." Ellie wasn't Paul's typical girlfriend, his preference was a woman who would understand him culturally and emotionally, therefore he would not have to explain the minutiae of his needs and moods and his experiences. With Ellie, the getting-to-know-you stage would be more protracted because of what he perceived to be cultural and social differences that were not readily discussed out of politeness and a desire not to offend. Before starting university, Paul had planned that he would be more adventurous and less restricted and was ready to widen his taste in friends and the relationships that he would pursue. University offered the perfect landscape where he could broaden his horizons and Ellie provided the reason for him to venture further afield in his quest for love beyond the type of partner that he had previously been drawn to.

Ellie was the product of Hazel Sackville and Norman Hayes. She was an only child and her parents never married. It was reason enough to burden their daughter with both their names to stop the village gossip and the snide remarks that the conservative minds of Risborough in Buckinghamshire would happily dish out. But the double-barrelled name was a moniker she disliked, a heavy burden that she was forced to carry around. She felt that her surname did not play into her individuality, but rather it represented a sticking plaster constructed out of her parents' guilt at not marrying at a time and a place when a pregnant woman not wearing a wedding ring was unacceptable. Risborough was a sleepy town with its fair share of old money and a few occupants living for the next wage packet. Hazel and Norman fell into the latter category; he worked as a farm hand and she in the town's supermarket as a checkout assistant. Ellie could not wait to get away from Risborough and its single, nondescript high street that grew ever more humdrum after each visit. The young Ellie developed a fascination for archaeology after a school trip to Stonehenge. It was then that she knew she had to leave Buckinghamshire in order to make her dreams come true. She wanted to leave Risborough far behind. She wanted, too, to lose the double-barrelled tag and what it represented; that it reminded her of her parents' attempt at creating respectability. She wanted to throw off the cloak of rural insignificance and find herself. As soon as was feasible after her A-level results, her bags were packed and she headed east to Paddington, to London and to university.

Ellie's first date with Paul turned into a second, then a third. By the fourth date, Ellie felt that she trusted Paul enough to invite him to dinner at her small student accommodation. She had already made up her mind that sex was not on the menu, regardless of what Paul might have wanted, or at least had hoped for. She wanted to get to know him better before taking the relationship further. Ellie had prepared a simple meal of spaghetti Bolognese with a bottle of red provided by Paul. The evening filled with conversation around books, favourite films, best childhood memories, a few tense rounds of truth or dare and laughter - lots of laughter. Ellie felt relaxed, secure, and attracted to Paul. Their conversational discourse slipped easily and slowly into kisses and caresses. It wasn't long before they were making love - despite her best intentions. Paul's eager intensity caught Ellie by surprise. She was sexually inexperienced, but she had been used to a gentler approach, a slow burn rather than an eager gallop, but she felt that she shouldn't say anything because of what Paul might think of her. She was living away from home for the first time and was caught in the dilemma that she will be thought of as someone who could not make the grown-up decisions about her life without having to justify them to her parents or grabbing the bull by the horn. Sex with whoever she fancied was one of those big, grown-up decisions she was looking forward to making once away from the social constraints of a small village. She felt Paul's eagerness, which she mistook for enthusiasm and a good sign that he was keen on her. Then came the heavy slaps, and the doubts and fears erupted in Ellie's mind, but she was also intrigued by the unexpected, edgy thrill mixed with fear that she was feeling, the control that she found herself struggling to maintain. It was like that first ride on a fast-moving, scary rollercoaster, a mix of fear and thrill, but she was uncertain of where it was leading to, the denouement presented itself as a dark and dangerous tunnel down which this now difficult ride was heading. She was no longer in control and had not welcomed this aspect of the sex act, but she quickly reached the conclusion that she did not like it. Rough sex was not for her. She wanted it to end.

The kissing, soft touches and gentle strokes turned into something more frenetic: Faster! Deeper! Harder! The Paul she thought she knew had been replaced by a complete stranger. "Stop!" Ellie demanded. She did not recognise Paul from the listening, caring man with whom she'd spent a lovely evening. He had left himself somewhere else. The slaps came more frequently and with more force, her cheeks reddening with each splayed palm landing on her bare buttocks, and the biting of the fleshy parts of Ellie's body became more intense, more painful. "Can you stop now Paul, you're hurting me?" Her assailant did not hear her cries and demands. He grabbed her by the throat and pulled her hair back, going as deep as he could, the sweat dripping off his forehead onto Ellie's exposed back. He was oblivious to Ellie's needs as he lost himself in his own carnal fantasy. She used all her strength to shake Paul out of his trance-like physicality and bring his violent lovemaking to an abrupt end. "Stop!" she shouted. Ellie felt uncomfortable and knew instantly that she had gone against her better judgement when she changed her mind and took the decision that evening to have sex with Paul. She immediately regretted it and decided that he was not what she wanted in a relationship – or even a friendship. He had manipulated the situation to his liking, she reasoned. Paul was told to leave, and Ellie took the decision there and then to delete Paul's number from her phone and vowed never to speak to him again. Thereafter, Ellie made certain that her movements around the university would not coincide with his, planning her lectures so that she would not meet him around the university campus. It was not enough.

What followed was a torrent of harassment: Paul turning up at Ellie's digs every night demanding to speak to her, Paul harassing her at every opportunity around campus, Paul trying to persuade Grace, her classmate and best friend at university, to pass on messages to Ellie that he was in love with her and could not understand why she did not want to see him again. She knew that the constant barrage of abuse would not stop unless she took matters into her own hands. That was when she vanished. Ellie did not tell friends that she was transferring to another university and did not tell them why, partly out of embarrassment and partly because she did not want Paul to know. She wanted him to live with the uncertainty of not knowing what he had subjected her to. A few months later Ellie sent Grace a message that she asked her to pass on to Paul. It simply read: "When a woman says stop, she means stop". Paul didn't understand.

"Any luck in finding Ellie Sackville-Hayes," Michelle asked Rebecca when they met. "No, not a sausage, but her name is quite unusual, it's only a matter of time before I track her down," Rebecca replied. "She's bound to be on social media, she must be. Everyone is." Michelle then had a flash of inspiration. "Why don't you search for Ellie Hayes, or Ellie Sackville. In the insurance industry we often get people with various versions of their name. They play around with their names because they take out multiple policies if they want to undervalue their possessions, which means they pay less of a premium. They see it as a way of saving money. People also play around with different versions of their names, normally involving other family members, if they want to stash away money from the tax man."

Picture This

Ray and Paul arrived at Ella's flat. It was late in the evening and the light was fading. Ray procrastinated and delayed deliberately, long enough for the evening to ebb away into dusk before they made their way to Brockley. He wanted the infrared surveillance cameras that he had installed to be working at their optimum. And for that, the darker, the better. As they made their way to the front door, Ray paused and reached for his pocket to retrieve his phone. "Oh, I've got to take this call. Ring the bell, Ella's expecting us." The trap was set. As Paul reached up to the bell, unbeknown to him, his actions were being recorded, and crucially, his hand. "Got you!" Ray smiled to himself, satisfied that his scheming had fallen into place. The next part of his plan was to put into action his concocted story of how he wanted to turn his work for the police into art and put on an exhibition of infrared images of people's hands, juxtaposing the idea of blood flowing through the veins with the changing topography of life. Ella opened the door and did not look at Paul, steering her gaze to her boyfriend and greeting him with a hug and kisses. She knew that she had to play the game, although it was a game that made her skin crawl to be so close to the man who was causing her such unnecessary pain and hurt. "I won't be long, just came to drop this off." Ray handed Ella a small package. He knew that she was uncomfortable meeting Paul but also understood that she had to. "Your favourite hand-made chocolates. They had to be hand-delivered. I wanted to show you how much I love you." The pair left without further discussion and made their way to the pub.

Their regular drinking venue was a short walk away from Ray's flat, and a guarantee of a seat was assured because of the vast outside space. "Two pints of your best IPA please." Ray took the opportunity to tell Paul about his latest "project" of photographing hands, carefully explaining to him the concept of how under infrared light, our hands take on the look of an abstract painting. "Yeah, I'm up for that. Where do I sign up?" Paul asked. A date was set for the hand photo session, and Ray knew that he would get a digital image of Paul's hands and therefore he would be able to match the unique signature prints with the images captured by Ella's CCTV cameras that he had installed. He had hoped that that would be enough grounds to bring a charge of harassment, but he was only too aware that to be taken seriously by the police, he would have to have stronger evidence. Harassment is a crime under UK law, but Ray wondered if having matching handprints added up to compelling evidence or entrapment, even though it puts Paul at Ella's place, being there does not constitute a crime. The Metropolitan Police routinely dismiss reports of burglary and car break-ins. A reduction in the police budget means that the priority is shifted away from what they see as petty crime, but what the victim experiences in such cases is a violent violation of their way of life. At that point, Ray knew that he had to do more, possibly take things into his own hands.

Ella was relieved that Paul was not in her space for longer than he needed to be, she immediately felt the tension lift as the two pals turned and made their way to the pub, and she was fully aware too, and thankful, that Ray did not prolong the uncomfortable uneasiness of having Paul at her doorstep. She satisfied herself knowing that at last her boyfriend was doing something, whereas before he would play down anything that was too challenging and uncomfortable. She knew that it was Ray's way of dealing with difficult situations. It was an aspect of conditioning, a way of dealing with trauma, and Ray's job meant that he would face the shocking realities of life's darker side every day, the same way A&E nurses anaesthetise themselves from the distressing day-in, day-out occurrences of a busy hospital. While Ella was not a psychologist, she understood why her boyfriend was always wearing his happy face, and she worried that underneath the accommodating demeanour, he was internalising the emotional trauma, the blood and gore. He saw this on a regular basis because he had observed enough of the wanton violence that his cognitive response was to process the abnormal behaviour in a way that enabled him to cope. She had picked up enough information about behavioural psychology from her mother, who was trained in the profession before giving it up to raise her family a few years after she married Ella's father. As a barrister, Ella's father could not see a reason why his new wife should continue to work when he was able to care financially for his family. Ella was concerned, though, that Ray would easily become immune to the repeated violence that he was exposed to. It was a concern that was always at the back of her mind. She also knew that to discuss Ray's coping mechanism openly could strip away his carefully constructed reality that enabled him to function normally when what he witnessed at work was anything but normal.

Doppelganger

Paul could not fathom why his relationship with Ellie had come to such a sudden stop. Her message that was passed to him by Grace did not, in his understanding, provide a proper explanation. He was left without answers, and even after the cryptic message from Ellie, he could not see why she would not have wanted to see him again. In his mind, he had given her what she wanted - a good time. Paul would spend the rest of his university days and the years that followed trying to make sense of his short-lived relationship with Ellie, a relationship that he would have liked to have turned into something more meaningful. But rather than shrug off the relationship as a learning experience, he chose blame. From that moment on he put the opposite sex and notion of romance behind him and threw himself into music and his studies, preferring not to leave himself open to what he perceived as being used by another woman the way that he thought that Ellie had used him. Paul resented being dumped so abruptly and finally, therefore seeing her as nothing more than an opportunist who used him to satisfy her own sexual curiosity, and when that had been satisfied, she'd discarded him without explanation or consideration of how he might feel. He vowed to one day find Ellie and exact revenge for the way that she had treated him.

When Ray introduced Ella to Paul, it set off a chain of events that took Paul back to his university encounter with Ellie. He became confused by the physical resemblance between the two women, and he became delusional, his thinking fixating on the belief that Ella was in fact Ellie; it was a viewpoint that did not fall in line with the reality of how everyone else saw the world. Paul could not distinguish between the past and the present, the two timelines became one: he was convinced that Ella was his short-lived university girlfriend, Ellie, and he set out on finding ways to prove that what he saw was the true reality. To Paul, Ellie and Ella had become one. What Paul could not understand was why Ellie had adopted a new name and why she was pretending that she did not know who he was, why she had erased him from her past. He vowed that he would get through to the person he saw as Ellie, who now from his version of reality, was calling herself

Ella, and why she was dating Ray, his best friend. And why Ray was playing along with everyone in pretending that Ellie had taken on a new identity and become Ella. The rejection by Ellie while Paul was at university got in the way of his ability to make sense of the situation that he found himself in.

Ella was determined that Paul would not prevent her from carrying out her normal day-to-day activities, but she knew that recent events meant that she had to be wary of Paul and be ready for anything. She was determined to continue to run, having set her goal on gaining an entry to the marathon, she knew she had to build up the miles in training in readiness of her taking part in what was for her going to be a massive achievement. As a precaution, she started to wear a special camera that recorded her runs. It attached itself securely to her a special harness worn around her chest as a security measure for when she was running by recording in hi-definition video if anyone was near her. After each run, she carefully studied each video footage, but it was the CCTV that Ray had set up that captured Paul posting something through Ella's letterbox that made her realise that her nightmare was not over. She opened the letter and started reading.

Dear Ellie

I don't know why you suddenly ended our relationship while we were at university, and furthermore, I find it confusing why you are now pretending to be someone you are not. What did I do wrong, please tell me, I'd like to know so that I can put it right. I know it has been a few years since we were together, but I felt that after making love that first time, we had something special. Seeing you again has awoken my deeply held desire for you.

Paul XXX

Ella gasped in shock and dropped the hastily scribbled letter on the kitchen table and reached for her phone. Rebecca answered and listened intently as Ella read the contents to her. "He obviously thinks you're his ex," said Rebecca. He's delusional. I'd be very careful If I were you. He knows where you live. Tell Ray, now!" Rebecca was now concerned about the safety of her sister and suggested that she either spend as much time at Ray's flat, or she will move in with her for as long as it takes. Rather than be afraid and having to change her lifestyle because of Paul's threatening behaviour, Ella decided that she'd confront the problem head on. Rather than running and hiding away, she'd face Paul's uncertainty and his irrational behaviour. She was determined not to shy away because she now realised that it was not a case of Paul not liking her, as she had thought. The chasm was much deeper and complicated than simply a case of two very different personalities running headlong into one another. Ella wanted to get back to a life without fear and anxiety, and she knew that to do that, she would have to strip bare Paul's tangled grasp of reality and hold it up to him like a mirror. Telling Ray of the latest intrusion into her life gave her boyfriend a reason to adopt a more considered approach regarding his relationship with Ella. He read Paul's letter with concern, but he did not have any answers. He knew that if he confronted Paul, he would be met with denials and counter accusations. He knew too that getting the police involved would not lead to anything until Paul commits a crime that could be prosecuted. He did not know what to do, but he knew that he had to do something to protect Ella from Paul.

"The letter is worrying, Ella, it suggests that Paul needs help, but he will fight against any accusation that he is ill, although clearly he is suffering from some sort of psychosis because he believes that you and his ex-girlfriend are one and the same person." Ray searched back through their time together, the nights out, the shared beers, the gigs… dragging up each memory looking for a hint or a sign that he may have missed that could have acted as a trigger for Paul's strange behaviour. As far as he knew, Paul did not do drugs, there was no evidence that he could recollect, although Ray could not account for what he did when he was with his musician friends given the casual approach to drug use among musicians. He thought that Paul was too clever to jeopardise his reputation and his ability as a musician to become involved in drug use. Ray realised that Paul did not have any close friends outside their relationship, and certainly there was no recollection of a relationship with another woman before or after Ellie. "You know him better than I do, Ray, but I have always felt that he didn't like me from the very first time we met. I always thought that he was emotionally cold and a little intense at times, when what he really needed was to let his emotions out, but he could be very closed. Would you agree, Ray?" Ray's response was to remind Ella that hindsight is a blessing. His concern was to focus on the present and how to get Paul to realise that Ella was not Ellie. Ray knew that he could prove that Paul was turning up at Ella's flat because he had the infrared handprint that provided a match that put him at the scene, but he could not risk his girlfriend's safety by confronting Paul, especially as his response would likely be one of denial in a concerted effort to further damage Ella's reputation.

Ella shared Paul's letter with Rebecca and Michelle because she wanted to get their opinion and an idea of what she could possibly do. "I think it would be a good idea if when we find Ellie, get the both of you to confront Paul so that he could see that you are different people, he will then leave you alone," said Rebecca. Michelle, though, was very clear about why she thought Rebecca's proposal would not work. "Sorry Rebecca', that's a dangerous idea, it could even worsen the situation. Ella is the trigger that has caused Paul to dredge up whatever caused him to respond in this way. There clearly was some sort of trauma around his relationship with Ellie, and we don't know what it is, and having the both of you stand in front of him will not likely have a good outcome. I suggest we find another approach to establish a solution to this." The three women put their heads together and soon realised that their collective expertise did not include diagnosing such complex cognitive behaviour that Paul was demonstrating. Ella then recalled her mother's nascent career as a psychologist and that it could prove useful in shedding some light on Paul's state of mind and why he had dangerously conflated his past life with Ella's present life.

Ella was initially unconvinced that her mother could help. It had been the best part of 25 years since she gave up her career to raise her family and support a husband that would ultimately leave her. Ella wondered if asking her mother to unpick her ongoing psychological battle with Paul would remind her that she gave up a promising career for her husband. But what did she have to lose? Ella was aware as a young woman that her father's way of supporting his family was to keep up the monthly payment that would keep her and her sister in school and the family in their five-bedroom house. Her father's income maintained a lifestyle that built a protective financial wall around the family. "Mum, I need to speak to you." Ella's call to her mother immediately set off alarms of concern in her mother's mind. "I'm on my way home, put the kettle on, I need to talk to you about something that has been bothering me."

When Ella arrived at her childhood home, her mother had brewed a fresh pot of coffee. As she sipped her warming black beverage, her mother listened to every twist and turn of the trauma that she had been put through over the past few months. Nicola was careful not to interrupt her daughter, recalling her training that in some situations it is better to listen than to judge. When Ella paused having brought her mother up to date, the psychologist retreated, and the mother came to the fore. She hugged Ella and realised that as a grown woman she could not always be there to offer a safe place for her daughter. A mother's instinct is always to protect her children, but there will always be occasions when the child must learn to cope with difficult situations themselves.

"He's showing classic signs of schizophrenia," Ella's mother eventually said. "It's typical of someone who is suffering from this type of psychosis to not be able to make sense of what is real and what isn't. Delusions can begin suddenly or may develop over weeks or months; and could take on a similar scenario that has presented itself here: Paul is creating his own misunderstood reality based on what he believes to be the correct version of events. It's an unfortunate coincidence that this poor girl has a striking resemblance to you, which is why Paul is unable to detangle what is real from what he imagines to be real. Something happened that has trapped his sense of reality in that time and place. The lying, the bullying and the constant harassment are not so much a sign of malicious intent – in many cases people who have psychotic episodes are not violent, just confused, delusional and show disorganised and erratic behaviour. Also, as you say, he doesn't see the two of you as the same person when you and Ray are together is strange, but understandable at the same time because Ray's and his relationship is rooted in a present reality that is linked to a shared past, therefore you become Ray's girlfriend whenever you are with him, but away from Ray, he sees you as this other girl. It's his way of managing his friendship with Ray. It's a different reality and in that reality, Ella is Ray's partner. The strong physical resemblance is probably all the trigger that he needs to see Ellie whenever he sees you alone, but to see you, Ella, when you are with Ray. Another trigger may be stress. The very fact of his relationships with Ellie ended abruptly, or his recollection of that relationship, in his mind did not work out for him because of the sexual and emotional dynamics. None of these things necessarily cause schizophrenia, but they can trigger an episode.

But the mind of a schizophrenic isn't linear and can be difficult to understand, let alone predict. He needs medical intervention, Ella, not punishment. Paul has become immersed in himself. And I would caution Ray against some sort of revenge out of a sense of protecting you. I would tread carefully. There are two men in your life who would do anything to protect you, go to any lengths: your father and Ray. Neither would see Paul as someone who needs help, rather, they will see him as someone whose actions should be avenged. Their love for you will translate into a rage-fuelled onslaught on Paul for what they will see as his transgressions. Neither man will see a sick individual who needs specialist medical help, what they will see is someone who needs a good going over. So, be careful what you tell Ray and your father, and more importantly, how you reveal the news of Paul's behaviour to either man."

Ella left her mother's house with a clearer understanding of what and who she was dealing with, and as a result, she felt less troubled, and with her mother's words echoing in her ear, she was more aware of the possibility of her father's or Ray's anger spilling over into an act of revenge. However, she still did not have a solution other than that Paul needs medical intervention. She felt that the only person who could convince him to seek help is Ray, but first she had to convince Ray that Paul needs help, and he would have to suppress his growing anger towards him and persuade him to see a doctor. And that would mean forgetting all his carefully constructed plans of trapping him like a criminal with his photographic techniques or persuading one of the known corrupt police officers to carry out a covert operation to punish Paul. The urgency of the situation was highlighted when Ella arrived back at her flat to another hand-delivered letter. Now, Ella was not convinced that she could rely on Ray to behave sensibly in trying to find a suitable solution to the ever-worsening situation.

Dear Ellie

I can only assume that the reason why you refused to see me after our night together was because you changed your mind about dating a black guy. I can only assume that I was being used to satisfy your sexual fantasy, which is how literature has portrayed women like you throughout the centuries. It is not ok for you to do that: to pull me in, to pretend you liked me, to make out that you wanted a grown-up relationship with me when all the time all you wanted to was to taste the forbidden fruit, and whatever fucked-up imagery of what that was supposed to represent. And then you drop me like a used paper cup after you'd tasted the forbidden fruit, and your refusal to answer my calls or see me was a slap in the face after what I remember as an enjoyable evening that ended in what was equally enjoyable love making.

And here you are years later pretending to be someone else, even changing your name, but I haven't been fooled, I know who you are. Your sudden disappearance left me highly stressed to the point that I began to blame myself for you leaving university. You owe me an explanation, Ellie, and I won't stop till I get one.

PS, I was falling in love with you. I found your gentleness and innocence endearing in a beautiful way that you don't often see in women who have not been spoiled and beaten

down to a point where they've become part of the negative
energy of the city and the way that we are forced to live our
lives in a society that does not reward people like you or me.

Paul.

After reading the latest of Paul's letters, Ella sighed
and realised how serious the situation was. However, she
was emotionally drained from listening to her mother's
learned and sensible explanation of Paul's behaviour. She
had planned to meet Ray for Sunday lunch at his place and
would show him Paul's letter then.

Summers in the UK are either a few glorious short
months of high temperatures, lazy, long balmy nights and
fond memories that remain the centre of dinner-party
conversations throughout the autumn and into the winter,
or they are a damp, wet, long disappointment. Fortunately,
this year the weather gods were smiling on Southern
England. Summer was at its most glorious. It was the type
of Sunday when Ella thought she'd walk to Ray's flat rather
than drive: the day was too lovely to be trapped inside a
motorised moving metal cage and the half-hour stroll
down to Lewisham gave her a chance to think about Paul's
latest distressing letter and how she would present it to
Ray. She remembered her mother saying that Paul needs
help, not punishment, and that Ray should be mindful of
that. Her mother's advice would be the way in which she
would broach the subject of Ray persuading Paul to see a
doctor.

"Hi Ella." Ray drew his girlfriend close to him. He was
hungry and eager to head to the restaurant. "Let's wait a
bit. I have something to show you," Ella said. Ray read the

letter at least three times, on the third occasion pressing his thumb and index finger into his temple. "Ella, I can fix this, don't worry. I'll make sure you don't hear from Paul again." Ella knew that her boyfriend's direct and firm pronouncement was not an idle threat and that it was within his capabilities to inflict severe harm on Paul, even if he would not be the one to inflict any punishment or harm. He had the contacts, and she knew from the anecdotal stories that they shared over breakfast that he would not find it difficult to ask the right person to do him a favour. "No, I don't want you to do anything to Paul. He needs help. I spoke to my mother, and I may not have mentioned it, but she used to be a practising psychologist before the three of us came along. She said Paul is suffering a psychotic episode and his behaviour is classic signs of schizophrenia. What she said, too, which I find interesting, is that Paul's behaviour has been triggered by some sort of trauma, which we'll never know about. You certainly won't hear it from him because Paul sees the world as perfectly normal, it's his version of reality. He won't, therefore, understand why you have turned on him."

Ray took in what his girlfriend was telling him and marvelled at her ability to see the good even in the most dire of situations, and especially when she was the target of the opprobrium. It was one of the many qualities that Ray admired in Ella. She would stop and talk to homeless men and give them money and food, regardless of whether they would misuse her generosity. She would spend Christmas Eve giving up her time to help at shelters that fed the homeless, and she would sponsor every neglected child if only she could afford it.

"Do you mean to tell me that you expect me to do nothing about this," Ray said, waving the letter in the air. "He needs a good beating; it might knock some sense into him." Sensing that she was possibly seeing a violent side to Ray that she had not previously witnessed, Ella swiftly pointed out the absurdity of Paul's conflicted mind in the way that he does not see her as Ellie when she is with Ray but transposes his ex-girlfriend on to Ella when she is not with Ray. "I don't get that at all. It doesn't make any sense on any level," Ray said. "Precisely," Ella responded. "Nothing makes sense in the way that they might make sense to you and me, but that's the apparent contradiction of schizophrenia: nothing makes sense but in the mind of the person who is having the psychotic episode, their version of reality makes perfect sense. Well, that's how my mother explained it to me."

The couple made their way through lunch without mentioning Paul's letter, though the revelation caused Ray great unease. On arriving back at his flat after lunch, they were met by a smartly turned-out figure dressed from head to toe in black. Ray and Ella smiled at Michelle, she returned the warm greeting, her unexpected presence acting as a welcomed intervention to the heaviness of the past few hours. "Can I borrow your boyfriend for a few hours, Ella? You'll be glad to know that this will be the last time: I have one more essay to write before I complete my masters." Inside Ray's flat, Michelle intuitively made a pot of coffee and filled three cups – no milk, no sugar. The friends sat down, Ray and Ella were careful not to say anything about Paul's letter, they did not want to detract from the reasons why Michelle had made her way to Ray's apartment.

Michelle pulled an A4 notepad from her bag and set a recorder on the coffee table in the living room. "You don't mind, do you, I really don't want to miss any expert snippet of opinion and insight. You both know what the subject matter of my degree is, but for this essay I want to explore the ideology of class being an instrument of control, but I want to take it further and talk about how language also acts as a means of control over non-whites, though it is quite clear that working class whites are also, unwittingly, subjected to this same degree of control as non-white immigrants to this country." Michelle read an excerpt from Orwell, a writer and social commentator that she had come to rely on to provide supporting evidence for her observed interpretation of the UK's class struggle as it is implemented today.

If you control the language, you control the argument

If you control the argument, you control information

If you control information, you control history

If you control history, you control the past

He who controls the past controls the future." – *Big Brother, 1984*

The afternoon's discussion centred around what Michelle termed as a deep sense of social control by successive governments, and how the deference to authority renders the working classes as a non-thinking, accepting mass who believes what they are told to be true and right. "When you take away a person's ability to rationalise and question what they have before them, they become metaphorically lobotomised, they lose the ability to think critically – and they will obey authority, whether that be the police or the politicians - even celebrities whose life is lived large on social media where the smallest indiscretion or gimmick is mimicked and applauded. This means they have no power over their own actions. Was it like this in Jamaica, Ray," Michelle asked? "Well, yes and no. You must remember that Jamaica takes a lot of its way of life from Britain, even the judicial system is still to this day governed and dictated to from London. The difference is the people are not, as you put it, lobotomised – well, not yet anyway. Jamaicans are known for their rebellious nature, we won't put up with what we don't agree with, and you can see it in the music of the island. Reggae lyrics form a sort of storybook of the way we live. You can hear stories, anecdotes, even the retelling of historic events. For example, if there's a hurricane, within days the reggae charts are full of songs telling every detail of how this person or that person overcame hardship, saved their house and their animals from certain death at the hands of the wind and rain, even personifying the event itself. You also have to remember that the class system is not as entrenched in Jamaica as it is here: we are a young country, and I'd like to think that we, even in our infancy, are more egalitarian, open, even classless, than the UK's entrenched, centuries-old system, which is based on and is built on the upper class using its privilege to control poor people. And you can extend that to the non-white people from all over the Commonwealth - even outside the Commonwealth, many countries fall victim to a style of colonialism."

Ella laughed at her boyfriend's elucidations and reminded him how enamoured he was of everything British when they first met, and she also took great pleasure in reminding him that it was she who lanced the boil of expectation of the Mother Country during the first flickers of their relationship. "And was it like that for you, Ella? Your experience of class and race must be very different to Ray's or mine, both of us being black. I imagine, too, that your experience and perspective of race and class must be very different from the white, working-class kids who went to school down the road from your privileged school?"

Ella paused before she responded to Michelle, admitting that she could only speak from a position of being a member of the very stratum of society that Orwell railed against, those whose position in society was an affront to Orwell and other social commentators, such as William Golding and Noam Chomsky. Ella's social class did indeed control the language, the history, the information and therefore the past and the future. Ella and her privately educated cohorts went on to the best universities and filled the top jobs. "I know I may sometimes come across to you two as an extra from the film Love Actually, but I think things are better than they were. And they are getting better with every passing generation, although we do tend to homogenise everything: every black person is African, ignoring the fact that there are more than 50 countries that make up that continent, and that mindset is transferred to the UK where everyone is thrown into the same melting pot. I suppose lumping everyone together is a subliminal form of control. It's easy, right? Fifty years ago, Ray and I could not have dated as openly as we do now, though I admit there's still a long way to go before people aren't judged because of their class and race. And equally, Michelle, you and Frankie would not be able to be so open about your relationship."

Michelle, though, wanted to wring every droplet of information out of her friends. "And how is language used by one race to disempower another race? I think that language is used as a tool, like a physical instrument that is used to silence opposing voices, voices of dissent or rebellion. The judicial system in colonised countries relied on the fact that the indigenous population would not understand the archaic and mysterious language of the law, which made it easier for plantation owners to wield enormous power over their slaves. Slaves were often accused and tried for the most trivial indiscretion and were not in a position to protest their innocence because they did not have the language to challenge the injustices that took place, they didn't even speak the same language as the plantation owners, and it is the same today when, although people can read, to a large extent, the masses, the working classes, do not have the educational sophistication and knowledge to understand how the language being used by the ruling class is keeping them from challenging the many injustices that is forced on them, sometimes without the poorest in society even realising it."

While Michelle was happy to continue exploring the academic discourse of race and class, Ella had other ideas, and was determined to steer the conversation to her own concerns. "Err, Michelle, this is all very well and worthy and academic and all that stuff, and I'm sure you'll get an outstanding response from your professor and be lauded from the rooftops, and sorry to rain on your parade, but we have something that we'd like to share with you, as you've been in on this from the start. Paul has written "me" a letter, which is, if not as, then more disturbing than the first letter." Ella reached into her handbag and handed Michelle the letter, which she read in disbelief.

"He's dangerous. Gaslighting is a form of psychological abuse, a mind fuck. He's messing with you Ella," said Michelle.

"No, he needs help, medical help," said Ella.

"That may be, but if someone such as Paul as much as sees the inside of a mental institution, it will definitely mark the end for him. Over-medication is a type of "cure" that will turn out to be his worst nightmare. The medicalisation of this otherness that Paul exhibits will not end favourably for him. He knows what he is doing to you and therefore someone needs to let him know it's not acceptable - at all," Michelle argued.

"No, he needs to be taken to a dark alley and severely dealt with," argued Ray.

"Has Rebecca located Ellie yet? Ellie's the only one who can tell us what the hell happened all those years ago," Michelle added. "Paul mentioned in his letter that the fact that he was black was the reason why the relationship came to a sudden end. Do you believe that Ella? I mean, to me it seems a flimsy reason to be so cut up after a break-up. If Ray and you broke up, or if Frankie left me, or vice-versa, would you resort to such extreme antics?"

To Ella it wasn't as simple as that. She understood that Paul was not well, in her estimation his behaviour was testament to that. What she was clear about, however, was that her apparent doppelganger held the key to unlocking the mystery of Paul's eccentric and disturbing behaviour. Ella called Rebecca, first to bring her up to date on what had been happening, but more importantly to find out if she had made progress on tracking down Ellie, who was proving elusive, causing Rebecca a modicum of panic because it was her firm belief that everyone leaves a footprint on social media, and no-one disappears because so much data is being collected on every citizen at almost every moment of their daily lives. "She's out there, Ella, I know she is. I just need more time." For Ella, though, she did not want to subject herself to Paul's unpredictable and traumatising interjections into her life any longer than was tolerable. She asked Ray if there was anyone else in their circle of friends who might know the whereabouts of Ellie. Ray could not, he recalls that Paul was very much one of the guys, and Ellie was the only girlfriend that he was aware of. "Ah! There was Grace, they always went around together, but I suppose you'll need more than a Christian name. Without more information it's just another needle in a haystack. Sorry!"

Finding Ellie was proving difficult for Rebecca. She used all her skills at navigating social media, even trying Michelle's suggestion of searching for Ellie Sackville or Ellie Hayes. She friended anyone who attended the same university as Ellie on every social media platform in the hope that by making as many connections as possible, Ellie's name would present itself, giving her the breakthrough that she needed. It was when Rebecca dispensed with the digital platforms available to her on social media and turned to more traditional methods of investigation that she began to make inroads in discovering Ellie's whereabouts. Her breakthrough came after she visited the offices of Births, Deaths, Marriages. From the records she discovered that Ellie Sackville-Hayes was born in a small town in Buckinghamshire. She learnt that she had not married and had not changed her name by deed poll. But annoyingly for Rebecca, her address was still listed in Risborough, but she was not there. But the apparent bad luck turned into an opportunity because it meant that she could visit Ellie's parents in the pretence of being an old college pal who is trying to reconnect with her. It was a ruse that she was not certain would work, she could only hope, but it was worth trying if it meant learning the whereabouts of the elusive Ellie Sackville-Hayes.

Ellie's parents did not question why Rebecca had unexpectedly turned up on their doorstep one early afternoon asking questions about their daughter. She was about Ellie's age, and knew where she studied, so Rebecca's story sounded plausible enough not to arouse suspicion. "You won't find her here, dear, she doesn't come home much these days because she's working in Leeds for The Council for British Archaeology. They're in the phone book, give them a call. But don't ask for Ellie Sackville-Hayes, these days she uses her middle name, Jessica, and my name, which is Hayes. She never did like having both mine and her dad's names. She always said it made her sound posh, and we are anything but. It was as if Ellie became a new person after she changed her course and university; It wasn't just the name change, it was as if she wanted to start over. I don't really understand her motives, but we are always there for her." Rebecca thanked Ellie's mother and turned on her heels allowing herself a congratulatory smile of satisfaction. At last, she felt that she was getting somewhere in helping her sister put behind her a difficult period in her life. On the train back to Paddington, Rebecca tapped "Council for British Archaeology" into her phone's search engine. The contact details came up, Rebecca saved them but resisted the temptation to call Ella with her good news. She didn't want to tell her that she had found Ellie, now known as Jessica. Not just yet.

Ghosts From The Past

"Look, I don't know who you are, and I have nothing to say to you. Please don't phone me again." It wasn't the reception that Rebecca had expected from Ellie. She had anticipated a cautious response, but she did not anticipate the abrupt conclusion to the phone call, a call that she thought would be the key to unlocking the secrets that this unknown woman had been keeping. Nor did she expect the unmistakable force of the refusal that emanated from Ellie. Rebecca had touched a raw nerve by mentioning her old university. She had resurrected a painful memory from her past. Rebecca accepted that she was a stranger to Ellie, and therefore she had expected a degree of suspicion because Rebecca presented as an unknown proposition, someone who she did not know. She thought about where she had gone wrong in her opening gambit. She carefully retraced her script. "Hi, my name is Rebecca. Did you go to university with someone called Paul?" The cold assessment of her words made Rebecca realise that she would have to adopt a different, gentler approach, one that was more considered and subtle. What that approach was, she did not yet know. Rebecca would have to either find a way to persuade Ellie to meet her, or she would have to force her to meet her. She preferred the former option, but she was ready to employ the latter in order to get Ella the respite that she knew she was desperate for.

Rebecca had allowed enough time to pass before she contacted Ellie again, but this time she was more circumspect. "Hi. It's Rebecca. We didn't hit it off the last time we spoke, but I need your help. I was given your name by a friend who attended the same university as you. I want to talk about Paul Robinson. I believe you knew him." Rebecca waited for Ellie's response. The pause was long and uncertain. "What did you say your name was," asked Ellie. "And who gave you my details?" Rebecca was prepared, quickly reminding Ellie of her credentials, and just as swiftly recalling the name of Grace that Ray had mentioned in a previous conversation. Rebecca reasoned that Grace was a reliable contact and that Ellie would therefore believe her. Rebecca was acting on a wing and a prayer - nothing more. The mention of Grace did, indeed, appear to put Ellie at ease, to the extent that she agreed to meet Rebecca. Her contact with Grace since moving to Leeds was limited to Christmases and the occasional phone call. Grace had since married and was living in West London. The two women's lives had progressed in different directions, though they kept in touch, albeit infrequently. But getting Ellie to meet her was only the starting point for Rebecca: the hard part would be to get her to open up about her past and more importantly, open up about what exactly happened between Paul and her. It would take planning, guile, subterfuge, and getting to know Ellie.

Ella, for her part, decided that after a long discussion with Ray, she would spend more time with her boyfriend given what they both now knew about Paul's fragile state of mind. The less time that she spent alone, the less chance of her encountering Paul while he was having one of his episodes, therefore keeping her safe. She did, however, resent having to curb her comings and goings in this way: she was not a victim and was not about to start behaving like one. "Paul is the one who needs to be on his guard, not me. Paul is the one who needs help, not me". These were defiant thoughts that Ella repeated to herself regularly. "Being careful costs nothing," Ella heard herself reciting one of her mother's many cautionary warnings. Along with her mum's proverbs, she put her concerns to one side. Paul, though, did not see the current situation in the same way that Ella, Michelle, Rebecca, and Ray did. Paul remained locked in his own conviction that Ellie was in fact masquerading as Ella and that she owed him an explanation as to why their relationship as he saw it come to such a sudden end - and without a clear reason why she had absconded without a word, leaving him to draw his own conclusions of the now damaged relationship. But Paul was full of resolve to get to the bottom of what happened that night. The fact that he may have been at fault escaped him. He simply couldn't understand what had gone wrong - even after the many years that had passed without any contact from Ellie.

The Gospel According To Paul

Paul's grasp of sensuality and lovemaking was naive, confusing, and ambiguous. As a young man he grew up always feeling as if he was the odd one out. In church he didn't fit in, and he would often question the religious constraints that the bellowing, imposing preacher that stood up at the pulpit every Sunday threatening brimstone and fire if any one of his flock dared to veer from the righteous path set out clearly in the good book. In school Paul felt uncomfortable around the girls in his mixed comprehensive. Consequently, he found the company of women challenging, not really knowing how to approach the opposite sex, let alone engage in meaningful conversation with women if they approached him. Women were a strange breed to him, so much so that his young adolescent self did not understand how to behave or act around them. Paul's nervous uncertainty around women carried over to adulthood and with it the inability to listen and therefore to understand the nuances and sensibilities of making friends with the opposite sex. Paul, because of the coruscating way in which he was often spoken to, did not develop the required skills to communicate effectively. Instead, his uncertain, nervous interpretation of how to communicate was based on his experience of being spoken to in a condescending way. The result was that Paul encountered an emotional full stop regarding his ability to love and be loved. It would have disastrous consequences, especially as a teenager when confusion about his sexuality accelerated, pushing itself to the fore. One of Paul's first experiences was with an unapologetically "out" boy in school. An explorative snog led to Paul questioning his sexuality. Was he gay? Was his awkwardness around women a sign that he was more attracted to people of his own sex than the opposite sex? He liked what he had experienced from the other boy at school. But that tentative introduction to teenage exploration of sex had planted the seeds of uncertainty that left him in a muddled, confused state that stayed with him into his early 20s, and was reinforced by memories of his baying Sunday school preacher who made it clear in his interpretation of the Bible that any divergence from "God's way" was not to be entertained. Paul heard the warnings of Leviticus 18:22, 20:13 so often that he imagined that he would go straight to hell if he allowed such perceived deviant thoughts to even enter his mind - even for a second. Homosexuality was interpreted as a sin, even though when the Bible was written, sexual orientation was not defined for men or women. Paul was left to his own devices when it came to uncovering his own feelings. As a developing teenager he did not have the required maturity or knowledge to understand the hormones rushing through him, and he felt too conflicted to speak to anyone about how he felt after that first kiss that had given rise to the battle that was emerging and had begun to play havoc with his fragile adolescence state of mind.

His date with Ellie was in reality a fight against his own nagging uncertainties about his sexuality, a persistent voice that he could not silence about how he viewed himself as a man, which led to constantly fighting a refusal to admit to himself that he harboured an attraction to a chiselled jaw and a defined six pack. It was something that he would not allow himself to admit to for fear of condemnation from the black community. He was aware he grew up in an atmosphere where homosexuality was a taboo subject that is only whispered about in condemning tones - if at all. Paul was all too aware of the early Jamaican hits of singers such as Beenie Man, Capleton, Sanchez and Sizzla, whose homophobic dancehall lyrics had attracted opprobrium in the more liberal media. He would examine these and similar lyrics for explicit and implicit meaning, searching for possible phrases or lyrics that were reimagined as sonnets, a carefully structured line that might give a hint as to what led the writer to put pen to paper and express these ideas in such a symbolic way. Paul hid these feelings of doubt and uncertainty from Ellie, and from everyone else, mainly because he did not understand the feelings himself, and was afraid of expressing how he often felt fearful that he would be judged. He wanted his first sexual encounter with a woman to be an affirmation that he was not gay or bisexual and that he had all his manly chromosomes in the correct order. But Paul's interpretation and understanding of "normal" sex was, for Ellie, simply an act of rape. It was this that upset her. Ellie believed, too, that she would not be believed if she reported Paul. She was convinced that somehow it would be seen that she had led him on, that she consented.... She reasoned that it would be her word against his and "men" would close ranks against her. What probably upset Ellie the most was that she had completely misread Paul's character. He was in her estimation an apparently cool guy who had turned into a monster without warning. She could not understand how he could not understand the word no and when stop means stop; and not see it as a green light to continue what she considered to be a physical assault.

Paul, though, simply could not see that he had behaved in a way that was unacceptable. As much as he tried, he failed to pinpoint the exact incident that led to Ellie's refusal to have anything more to do with him after their date. He reasoned that Ellie broke off their relationship because of what could be any one of multiple reasons - but none of them that pointed to how Ellie felt during and after what Paul considered to be a consensual sex act.

Chasing Strangers

After agreeing to meet with Ellie, Rebecca boarded the 10:00 train from King's Cross heading to Leeds. It was a journey that she was looking forward to, but at the same time a journey that she viewed with nervous trepidation. While Rebecca was keen to get some answers that would once and for all unlock the mystery of what happened between Ellie and Paul, she was also fearful and anxious that Ellie would once again slam the door in her face for fear of dredging up an episode from her past that she'd happily prefer would remain buried. Rebecca knew, though, that this was not the time to begin to question herself, or the motives of wanting to uncover what by all accounts so far had been a traumatic period of Ellie's life. She knew, too, that to tease out of Ellie an accurate account of what happened, she would possibly have to lie, or at least, be less than forthcoming with the truth about why she wanted to meet with her. At that moment she understood why and how politicians can appear on television and in front of the media and effortlessly and skilfully say a lot without saying anything that could be interpreted as a clear and unambiguous message. She would have to be as guarded and skilful with her language when talking to Ellie in the same way that members of Parliament are circumspect when speaking to the press.

The reality was that Rebecca would have to construct an elaborately spun, far-fetched story, which made her feel guilty as it was another woman who was going to have the wool pulled over her eyes, who was once again going to find herself in the position of being on the receiving end; and Rebecca was in this instance the baddie. Her actions were contrary to everything that Rebecca believed in. She thought of herself as a feminist and as such found it contradictory that she would be deliberately hiding her true intentions from another woman. But Rebecca's insecurities about her intentions returned and she could barely console herself in the widely held opinion among academics that women make better liars than men, and that men usually lie when they want something, whereas women lie to hide uncomfortable truths. But there was a rationale in her thought process. Rebecca convinced herself that it was the right thing to do under the circumstances, despite a strong belief that her actions were going against everything that she believed in. She reasoned that by not telling Ellie the truth, that she wanted to know what happened between Paul and her, she would be protecting Ellie's feelings.

As the train rumbled northwards, Rebecca gazed out of the window, the countryside rushing past in a changing blur of greens. It was then that she became all too aware that Ellie, too, can hide the truth, and with good reason. She had, after all, adopted a different personality, now calling herself Jessica and ditching her family name to a shortened version that would erase any imprint of her past. She had trusted her feelings, trusted her date, and opened herself up to the possibility of a relationship only to have it thrown back in her lap in the most violent way. Hiding behind the truth by telling a little white lie is for some a coping mechanism, a survival strategy that acts as protection in times of need. She was also aware that Ellie might not want to recall the events of her encounter with Paul as a way of protecting herself against the negative feelings such recollections would inevitably bring up, feelings Rebecca reasoned, no woman in their right mind would want to be reminded of. The doubts of getting any sort of cooperation from Ellie surfaced again as Rebecca concurred that the reason why Ellie had created a new persona to protect herself, empower herself and rebuild her mental health and her self-esteem that had hit rock bottom, was to move as far away from anything that would remind her of Paul as possible. Rebecca was treading on unsteady ground - and she knew it.

As the train pulled into Leeds City railway station, Rebecca alighted and navigated her way to the imposing main concourse of the modern building that reminded her of a giant cream-coloured waffle interspersed with concrete and glass that made for an incongruous mix of old and new. She quickly looked left, then right and left again, her eyes fixing ever so briefly on every face that she thought could be Ellie's. She was eager to spot Ellie before she herself was spotted. She wanted to be able to occupy the higher ground, though she acknowledged that these feelings were nothing more than a nervous reaction that had its roots in uncertainty fuelled by the unfamiliar. But Rebecca somehow felt that it would give her the advantage. It was as she was looking in the near distance that she heard someone call out her name. It was Ellie. "Hi. I'm Rebecca. How did you know who to look for?"

"You were looking around like a frightened rabbit so I figured it must be you. Most people who come to Leeds either live here or know exactly where they're going. And you were so busy looking around in confusion, it didn't look as if you had home knowledge or that you knew where you were, let alone where you were going, so I thought it most definitely must be you."

"Oh. I had no idea that I was so easy to spot in a crowd," Rebecca responded.

"Only in Leeds City Station," Ellie laughed. "Let's have a coffee, I understand that you've got to catch the train back to London, so in my estimation, we've got about three hours. So, what do you want to know about me? I called Grace and spoke to her at length. I'm not a fool, Rebecca.

Grace and I worked out that you probably want to know about my brief relationship with Paul. Am I right? "

"Well…yes." Rebecca launched into her prepared speech, one that she had been rehearsing for days. She was determined not to make the same mistake as before and go bundling into another *faux pas*. "I'll get straight to the point. I have a friend called Ray, he's actually my sister's boyfriend, and he knows your friend, Grace. They went to the same university, as I believe you did too, well, initially, anyway. And Paul. So, here I am. Small world, isn't it?"

Ellie sensed that she was being manoeuvred ever so gently into a corner but decided that she would play along with Rebecca to see where her story was going and how it would unfold and if it would be necessary to tell Rebecca the whole truth. "Paul, your old boyfriend, has been harassing my sister, Ella, who is Ray's girlfriend, as I mentioned. Actually, it's more than harassment. He, Paul, that is, believes Ella is you masquerading as someone else. You see, Ella bears a striking resemblance to you, and as a result, Paul is becoming more unhinged, more delusional to the point of being dangerous. So, we want to find you to find out why he's getting the two of you so mixed up."

After listening to Rebecca, Ellie had heard enough. "I'm not sure I can help, really. Er, what was the name of your sister's boyfriend?"

"My sister's boyfriend? It's Ray, or Raymond to give him his full name, but everyone calls him Ray."

"I only have a vague recollection of him. Describe him for me."

"Geeky, happy-go-lucky, always smiling, smart but would often give off the impression that he wasn't, not bad looking, six-foot..."

"Mmm! No, sorry. Not the person that I had in mind. No, I cannot recollect anyone that fits that description."

The two women chatted - Rebecca choosing her every word very carefully trying not to spook Ellie, while Ellie responded to every inquiry guardedly. Time edged by, the awkwardness between Rebecca and Ellie was apparent, but both women were too polite and too careful to upset the other one with a misplaced word. Before Rebecca knew, it was time to catch her train back to King's Cross. They exchanged telephone numbers and promised to keep in touch. Rebecca settled back into her seat and replayed the conversation between her and Ellie in her head a thousand times and asked herself if she would ever be able to get behind an exterior that had been so carefully and skilfully put in place. Ellie appeared to Rebecca like an impenetrable coat of armour that was designed to keep prying questions at bay. She told herself that a strategy of softly, softly would prevail in the long term rather than trying to badger and force Ellie into telling her all that she wanted to hear about her time with Paul. She knew that if she pressed, Ellie would simply clam up and refuse to see or speak with her again.

A week had passed before Ellie called Rebecca. Rebecca had not been expecting to hear from Ellie so soon. However, feeling embolden, she took the chance to try and engage her further. "I must apologise for expecting you to remember Ray. He said you weren't around much after the Easter term of the first year. He wasn't sure what happened to you but said he believed that you left college rather abruptly and without telling anyone, so it's a bit unfair of me to expect you to remember him. Thanks for calling me back so soon."

Rebecca hung up quickly. She wanted to leave the information where she had planted it in the hope that Ellie would take the hint that she knew more than she was letting on and therefore allow Ellie to come clean about her past. She knew, too, that Ellie now knew that Rebecca had guessed that there was a good reason why she had left university suddenly. Rebecca was hoping it would be enough for Ellie to open up about Paul. It wasn't long, though, before Ellie called Rebecca, as she had hoped. Minutes after ending her conversation with Ellie, Rebecca lifted her phone to her ear.

"Hi Rebecca, it's Jessica - or Ellie, as you've been calling me. So you know, I am now known as Jessica, not Ellie. That was a former incarnation of me. I have decided to tell you my side of the story because of Paul and what he appears to be doing to your sister. I'll explain everything to you in person. I'll be in London for work for about five days starting next Monday. It will give us a chance to get to know each other a little better. When can we meet?" Rebecca had the opening she had been patiently waiting for. She excitedly hoped that "everything" really meant everything because she was running out of ideas of how to break down the carefully constructed defence that Ellie had built around herself over the past few years.

"How do you take your coffee?" Ellie asked Rebecca. The two women had decided to meet at a time and place that was convenient for Ellie's schedule. An eatery at London Bridge, overlooking the river Thames and with views to the Tower of London was the agreed location. "I was holding back when we met in Leeds. There's much more that I should have told you, but I was unsure of you and uncertain about your motives. You'll understand after I explain. I do remember Ray. I was raped, but I am sure you understand that I didn't want to be reminded about it. Besides, it remains my word against his. An allegation, nothing more."

"Ray?" gasped Rebecca in shock. "No, his friend, Paul. I remember Ray exactly how you described him. No, I wouldn't imagine Ray to be anything other than a gentleman. But Paul... We had been out a few times and it was going well, or so I thought. He seemed like such a nice man. Erudite, knowledgeable about a lot of things - even charming and funny, and fun at times. So, I thought I'd invite him round to mine for dinner. I think it was our third or fourth date, but really, it was only dinner, nothing more was on my mind, I'm not sure what was on his mind, but after a few drinks, things got out of hand, the evening careered out of control and I suddenly felt trapped. It all happened far too quickly. I didn't know what to do. I was scared, terrified, in fact. The police don't tend to take these allegations seriously, so I didn't report Paul, I just upped and left; I made up a plausible reason for my tutors and transferred to another university. I started to use my middle name, Jessica, from that moment on, I suppose it was a way of putting everything behind me, wiping the slate clean. New uni, new me, new start... you know. Maybe you don't. But now, years later, after meeting you and the fact that you mentioned that Ray remembers me leaving university abruptly, it occurred to me that Paul will likely go on to abuse other women - and I realised that I need closure. It seems that your sister might be a target, and possibly because of her resemblance to me. I can't have that on my conscience. So now you know what happened between Paul and me."

Rebecca understood that any type of sexual assault is difficult to talk about, so she chose her words with care as she explained what Paul had been subjecting Ella to and how, with Michelle and her help, Ella had been determined to put a stop to Paul's threatening and intimidating behaviour. Ellie was surprised on hearing what had been taking place and the way Paul seems to have been subjecting an innocent woman to his distorted sense of what he considers to be real. Ellie was particularly disturbed by how Paul had seen the similarities between her and Ella as somehow her pretending to be someone else. However, with the help of Rebecca's considered explanation, she could understand how a schizophrenic could conflate the two women. She understood, too, how the confused situation Paul had found himself in had obviously led to a lot of discomfort for Ella.

Ellie, though, remained resolute that there would be no benefit to either of them if they were to meet in person. "I don't want to meet Ella - I would find it too traumatic, too difficult, although she is as much of a wronged party as I am in this horrible episode. Besides, I'm sure your sister would find the whole thing a little surreal. It would be like looking at a version of yourself from a parallel reality. It would be too weird for both of us. So, no. Just hearing about it now makes it sound as if the whole thing was made up. I know that you suggested that it would be helpful if we both confronted Paul, but I think that could create an unpredictable situation that could set off a range of responses in him. By the sounds of it, he probably isn't mentally stable enough to comprehend what he'd be witnessing. The sight of the two of us might send him into an episodic spin that he might not recover from. Besides, I certainly don't want to meet him again. I have managed to keep him out of my life, if not my memory, for years, and I don't want to be reminded of what happened in close-up. I am angry that I felt at the time that I wouldn't be believed simply because I had invited him round to my place for dinner. It would be his version of events against my version of events. I am angry that I was made to feel so alone, so isolated. I am angry that complaints like mine are not taken seriously by the authorities - or by anyone in authority. I am angry that I have had to make massive, life-changing adjustments to the way I live to continue to function as a normal person, while all the time this man carries on oblivious to the impact his actions had on me. I am angry! So, I hope that you, Ella and your friends understand why I don't want my past to further impact my future. But more pressingly and importantly, what are you and your friends going to do about this weirdness that you are living through now that you know what happened to me and why I moved on?"

"I don't know what we are going to do," said Rebecca. "Paul doesn't see that he has done anything wrong, so, it will be difficult to press charges, especially as you would have to prove that a crime was committed; and to make matters worse, the incident is historic, which is mad, but that's the law as it is interpreted by our lawmakers. The safety of women is not something that society seems to take seriously, and the law does very little to protect women. Society has a very fixed idea of what masculinity is, what it stands for and what it represents. But I digress. The apathy of our legal system regarding women's rights is probably not something that you want to hear about given that you suffered brutally at the hands of this man and was let down by a system designed to punish women while men swan around unaccountably, but if Paul believes that Ella is actually you, pretending to be someone else, she is in danger. We must get him to see that you are two different people, but that might be too much of an ask for a schizophrenic with a flimsy and tangled grasp of reality. Michelle, our friend who has been supportive of Ella during this whole episode, and especially Ray, think that Paul should be dealt with, punished in some way, but Ella believes that Paul needs specialist help."

"And what do you believe Rebecca?"

"I don't know what to believe any more. Do you punish or help someone like Paul? Does he deserve help in view of what he did to you, or should he be punished? Both perhaps? Is there a case for more education and rehabilitation so that men like Paul understand that when a woman says no she means no? Is Ella correct in her assertion that we as a society don't take the time to sift out people with clear mental illness from those who simply have bad intentions? I'm sorry to have dragged up your past, Ellie, and I can appreciate that it must be unpleasant, but I must put my sister's wellbeing at the forefront of whatever I do. And Paul must pay, somehow, for what he did to you and what he is doing to Ella.

"Ellie, I mean Jessica, you have been as incredibly forthcoming as you possibly could with information relating to Paul and your brief - and horrifying for you - past together. It couldn't have been easy. And I understand if you feel as if you have given all that you are able or willing to give because of the distressing memories that have been resurrected, and I understand, too, if you want to return to the carefully constructed persona of Jessica. Ellie was someone you once were. I get that, I really do, but I hope that you understand that without your side of the story, Paul's behaviour doesn't make sense. What you have told me was the missing part of the jigsaw, the crucial corner of the puzzle that will enable Ella to get on with her life without having to constantly look over her shoulder, without having to always question her state of mind. This doesn't help you, I know, but I hope you understand."

Over the course of the next few weeks, Rebecca and Ellie spoke to each other about her past, about Paul and about her feelings. "It has been painful for me to speak so openly to you about what happened between me and Paul, but I realise that it's time that I find closure, and you telling me about what he is doing to your sister has convinced me that remaining silent, hiding in the shadows of my own mind, is not helping anyone - especially me and your sister. You now know everything, Rebecca. I have nothing more to say to you."

The two women had found friendship in adversity and had managed to cut through Ellie's suspicions and what at first appeared to be the uncertain intentions of Rebecca. But it was time for Ellie to let go of her past and time for Rebecca to return to her sister with the information that she had worked so hard to assemble. They met for the final time. As they stood in a small café in London King's Cross train station, Ellie gave Rebecca a smile that told her unequivocally that this was the last time she would hear from her. Ellie stood up, leaving her now nearly cold coffee, the cup half empty, on the small table in the corner of the café, adjusted her coat and waved goodbye to Rebecca knowing that whatever happens between Ella and Paul, she would not be part of it. Rebecca understood too that the Ellie that everyone knew from the past no longer existed. Ellie at last felt that she would finally be able to put the traumatising episode of what happened between Paul and her into a secure part of the recesses of her memory where it would stay forever. She felt certain that Ella had the measure of Paul, something that at the time she regretted not having the strength to do, believing instead that she was somehow at fault, that she had given Paul the wrong impression, maybe leading him on. It took a lot of soul-searching and many hours of counselling to understand that she was not the victim in their brief but painful encounter. She had no desire or inclination to see Paul again. He had taken away a part of her life that should be treasured and remembered for all the right reasons: the parties, the new friends, the experiences that you can only get from the closed biosphere of university life.

Unbeknown to Ellie, her view of Paul was the polar opposite of how Paul remembered their time at university. In his state of mind, Ellie was still very much entwined in a part of his own version of reality, his experiences, his future even. He could not let go of the memories - his memories. He wanted nothing more than to rekindle a friendship or even a relationship with Ellie when he returned from New York.

Opportunity Knocks

London. Midweek. A subterranean club tucked behind heavy black doors. A hidden corner of Soho that houses an exclusive, exciting nightspot. On the outside, a nondescript barely noticed aperture on the narrow but busy intersection of Old Compton Street and Frith Street. Inside, it was a buzzing club. Paul was caressing a tumbler filled with aged cognac while waiting to go back on stage for his band's second set when he felt a hand on his shoulder. "Paul, right? The bass player? I was listening to you earlier. Impressive! You know your way around your instrument."

Paul gazed up at the stranger who was complimenting him. "Thanks for the kudos. Appreciated. And you are?"

"Oh, I apologise. My name is Conrad. Conrad Smith. I'm an agent and I am here tonight as a guest of a friend, the person who is the promoter for this gig, but I'm not supposed to be working, but in reality, I am always working. You know how it is, right? Which brings me to the point why I would like to speak with you."

"Sorry mate, I'm due back on stage in a few minutes. Let's chat afterwards. OK?" Paul gulped down the remainder of the rich, dark beverage that he had been swirling around his tumbler, the chunks of ice melting slowly. Paul carefully negotiated the three steps that led on to the stage, steadied himself and grabbed his base. He was ready.

An hour later Paul wiped away the sweat from his brow. He reflected on his night's work and was pleased. Happy with the way the notes floated from the taut strings of his instrument and meshed with the syncopated beats of the drummer and danced with the sound reverberating from the lead guitar. Paul had hit every note perfectly, his musicality danced an exquisite back and forth with the piano player.

"That was brilliant," Conrad said. Yeah, Not bad," came Paul's measured reply. Conrad Smith, though, reasoned in his opinion that what he had heard and witnessed was exactly what he was looking for. Working or not and wherever he was, Smith always kept half an ear out for a bass player after being put on alert by the casting agency in New York that he was associated with. The brief was simple: a good all-round musician, adaptable, able to write music. Conrad, though, was expecting to find the type of musician that he was looking for in New York, not London. Smith had a good ear for music. He was someone whose abilities did not match his ambition. He fell in love with playing drums after being mesmerised on seeing Elvin Jones at a gig in Manhattan. But Conrad's journey from playing in a local garage band in his native Connecticut to the biggest stages in the world didn't happen. As much as he tried, he soon came to accept that he did not have half the dexterity of Jones to make it as a top drummer. But he was consumed by music and dedicated himself to finding the next best having accepted that he would not be that person.

"Paul, I have been scouting for a production company in New York. You fit the bill, and my friend who invited me down here says you are an all-rounder, able to turn your musical skills to a range of things. You are exactly what my client is looking for. Here's my card. If you fancy a change of scenery, call me. I fly back to the States in a couple of days. I expect your answer before I leave."

"Yeah, sounds good. I'll call you for sure." In the taxi taking Paul back to his flat, he pondered on the proposal. "A stint in New York could get me out of this rut, out of the suffocating atmosphere of London, time to clear my head, and a new start. And a chance to forget the idea of expecting Ellie to magically come back into my life, especially as she's pretending to be someone else and refuses to reconnect with me. Why not New York? The gig sounds too exciting an opportunity to pass up." Paul reached deep into his pocket for the half-crumpled business card. He squinted in the back of the cab, straining to focus on Conrad Smith's number through a fog of alcohol, tiredness and the tinted windows of the cab. He focused and dialled the number on the card.

Three weeks had passed, and Paul had been working in New York for the past two weeks after giving himself a week to find a flat and acclimatise himself with the area and meet his would-be colleagues. He liked what he saw and was hoping that weeks would extend to months. He hoped that this assignment would overrun by months. He was there for an important assignment that would put him in contact with key people in the music and publishing business that could set him up for life, so he knew that his skill as a musician and the chameleon way that he had with people would have to be at its best if he was to impress and charm the movers and shakers of the production company that he was working for. His job was simple; to write the music for a television series that was in its early stages of production. The carrot for doing a good job was more work - and what Paul saw as the possibility of a permanent move to America. He liked his new working environment and hankered for a move to the United States, and especially the Big Apple, although he couldn't fathom out why it was called such. An everyday fruit in no way captures the vibrancy of New York. Maybe it was the bewildering variety of the different kinds of apples that somehow had become a well-worn metaphor for the myriad types that march up and down the wide and bustling streets of Yonkers and Brooklyn, Harlem and Manhattan, Chinatown and Queens. Paul was determined to become famous in NYC. "If you can't make it here, you can't make it anywhere," he thought to himself before wondering, the thought juddering staccato-like through his mind. "Was it Frank Sinatra or John Steinbeck who said that?" It was a question that Paul didn't bother to sift through his encyclopaedic knowledge bank of song lyrics and popular phrases to find the answer.

"I love this town. The energy and the buzz are amazing. And with five different boroughs to explore, there's enough to keep me up all night while I am here. I only wish that Ellie was here to share it with me. Maybe one day we can be together again - in America - now that she is living in London. I just have to persuade her that what we had at university was real and get to the bottom of why she is pretending to be someone else, and why she left me so suddenly. But that can wait. Now, I want to enjoy this gig, enjoy these amazing musicians and equally amazing creatives, and enjoy New York. I have heard that Paradise Club and Mission are places to be. I think I'll check out the Barracuda Bar and Hardware too. But I mustn't get too carried away with the hedonistic side of the city. But there's also Birdland and the Blue Note Jazz Club to check out." It was during one of these many Saturday night let-your-hair-down clubbing sessions that Paul and Andre had first agreed to go out on the town together. Andre was a native New Yorker and part of the production team. His role was that of the Grip, the person whose job it was to set up all the equipment to support the cameras on set. Andre had to ensure that the rigging that allows the camera to move around the set was secure, the camera dollies, cranes, tracks, and camera setup were all fixed. The production company could not afford any messy accidents and the inevitable protracted wrangle with overly concerned insurance operatives. Andre's job was an important one.

Andre had befriended Paul, realising that he was not a local and reasoned that him being so far from home needed looking out for, if not looking after. Andre was single, which for him was rare. He was a regular on the New York gay scene, and his relationship status of being single never lasted too long. For Andre, though, an idea of a relationship was anything that lasted more than a month. His boyfriends didn't last much longer. If anyone got too close and the sex too routine, it was a signal for Andre to move on. If Andre had marked Paul out as a temporary distraction in his hedonistic lifestyle, Paul was not aware of it. His focus was on writing music. "All Cows Eat Grass", was a mnemonic that Paul kept repeating to himself as a reminder to that he must always emphasise the lower musical notes as he tried to match the music to the dialogue from the writers of the television series. Paul would often be heard mumbling A,C,E,G, repeatedly to himself.

It had been a hard day. Paul was surprised how committed these Americans were when it came to work. He was used to taking breaks every few hours, be it coffee or just a chance to chat with a colleague. But in New York, the work ethic was strong, and the entire team was accustomed to working a ten-hour day, often without breaks. Late into the evening, a Manhattan bar was where the boys found themselves, beers were followed by shots. It was agreed beforehand that Birdland was where they would see out the rest of the night, listening to jazz while soaking up the history and tradition of one of New York's finest jazz venues. Paul kept an eye on the bass player, following his rapid hand movements up and down the bass fretboard, soaking up every nuanced note change. "Do you like it here," asked Andre. "Yeah, it's brilliant, so alive. The musicians are amazing, I can't get enough of it," Paul responded. "No, I meant New York, its nightlife, not the club," Andre laughed, recognising that Paul was oblivious to anything other than the musicality that he was absorbing inside Birdland. "Are you seeing anyone Paul?" Andre's question was loaded with intent, but it did not get a response. Andre found Paul enigmatic and interesting, and attractive enough to show an interest in him. What he was not sure about was Paul himself. He had been observing Paul from a distance while the two men worked on set. He saw how easily Paul slipped in and out of conversation with both men and women. Andre observed, too, that Paul was particularly fond of Caitlin, the assistant producer. Andre reasoned that Paul's interest in Caitlin was due to her position on set and whatever influence she may have in putting in a good word for him when the time came. Andre was also aware after talking with Paul that he was keen to extend his stay in the United States, and possibly to Los Angeles and Hollywood.

As Andre returned to the table with more drinks, Paul blurted out excitedly, "did you notice how easily and skilfully the bass player manipulated his fretboard. Who is he? Is he famous?" Andre found the question sweet if a little naive. "Paul, in New York, every musician is at the top of their game. Some outstanding players never get noticed beyond the next gig. Every musician in this town is exceptional. They must be. To get on in New York you must have connections - and not just connections, but the right connections." As the two men emerged from the club and into the Midtown Manhattan night, Paul left the club drunk with excitement at the level of musicianship that he had just witnessed. "Do you want to get a nightcap at my place," asked Andre. "You can stay the night if you want, my apartment is in the Theatre district, so we really don't have far to go." Paul's reply was definitive. "No thanks. I want to head back to my place and absorb what I have just experienced." Paul at that moment had not attached any implied meaning to Andre's request. His head was full of the notion that he had been in the same club as some of the greats. Stan Getz, Charlie Parker, Miles, Dizzy Gillespie, Lester Young, John Coltrane, Monk and, more importantly, one of his idols, Charlie Mingus. Paul was aware, though, that the physical venue in which he had been enraptured by this no-name bass player was the new location of the club since 1985, but it did not matter to Paul; it was the name and the history of Birdland that resonated with him. "I've got a busy day tomorrow and I want to have a clear head. Thanks for the offer, but no thanks. See you at the office in the morning, and thanks for a great evening, Andre." The two men departing, each going in opposite directions. Andre would be home in a heartbeat while Paul started waving wildly trying to attract a yellow cab. Paul pushed Andre's invitation to stay the night to the back of his mind while Andre climbed the stairs to his apartment still uncertain about the sexual ambiguity that surrounded Paul. As the weeks rolled on, the two men continued their weekend tour of Manhattan's night spots - the gay bars, the jazz clubs, the Indy haunts... They became friends at work and away from work. Andre continued to push Paul's buttons, but without success, while Paul remained closed, keeping his sexuality buried as much as he could. He enjoyed Andre's company but was afraid to respond to the nagging voices in his head. He did not want to reach into his carefully suppressed emotions where Andre was concerned. Paul was reluctant to confront the doubts and the guilt that he had been battling with for as long as he could remember. He wanted to focus on his work.

Weeks had gone by and the production of the series was on schedule. The company was hearing positive noises on the media grapevine that the leading television companies were interested in bidding for exclusive broadcast rights to the series after seeing the rushes. Paul knew that he had satisfied his brief of writing music to fit the images and the story. He was pleased with his work, the fellow musicians on set were happy with what he had produced, and Caitlin, too, made it clear that Paul's contribution to the success of the production had been appreciated and noted. The two had grown closer after many weeks of Monday morning production meetings where small tweaks were made to the shooting schedule, each of which was accommodated with a willing smile from Paul. His work ethic and musicality had not gone unnoticed. He had worked hard, putting in the hours, absorbing the stresses that come with working in television production, something that he was not used to while gigging in London. Being on stage on the London circuit was easy compared with being so involved with the musical direction of a TV series. He was stressed, but in a good way. "Hey, Paul, fancy a drink after work?" asked Caitlin. "I'd love to," Paul replied with eager relish.

Caitlin was age 30 and considered it an ideal age. To her, your early 20s is all about exploration, your late 20s is about consolidation, but as soon as you turn 30, you have arrived. For Caitlin, the comfort of normal did not sit easily in her psyche. She was independent and ambitious and divorced from Bradley after two years of marriage, a liaison that in retrospect was too hurriedly undertaken. Caitlin and Brad had met at university, courted, and married. He wanted a family, she wanted Hollywood. It was never going to end on the same page. Caitlin had been single for the past four years and was wedded to her job. She had mapped out a career path for herself and reasoned that she would be a leading producer by the time she was 32. Brad did not share Caitlin's vigour, spirit, enthusiasm nor career pathway. After their marriage, he had settled into a cosy, well-paid job on Wall Street. A luxury apartment in Midtown Manhattan was a signal to the world that he had arrived. He didn't want much more. Caitlin, though, was not the settling type and their relationship quickly fell apart, both realising that they wanted different things in life: for Brad that was a wife, job, family, and a fancy apartment. For Caitlin, it was a walk on the wild side of life, exploring possibilities and getting to know the unknown. Divorce seemed the sensible path for both. Caitlin had learnt on social media that Brad had remarried: a fellow trader whom he had met at work. Game, set and match, Caitlin thought. The fact that her ex had remarried was not a source of regret, but rather a reason for celebration. At last, Caitlin felt an unshackling that the divorce alone did not give her. She was now truly free to do whatever she wanted to without fear of being judged by cutting comments and posts on social media or being pilloried by her peers for walking away from someone else's vision of perfection. Part of that freedom meant dating who she wanted and when she wanted. She had had her eye on Paul since he arrived in New York. She was attracted to his work ethic - and the fact that he was exotic: not American, not white. She knew very little about British men and even less about black British men beyond what she had read and what she had heard from her more adventurous girlfriends. But as liberal as New York is, race remains a divisive topic and a relationship with someone outside your culture was a taboo subject in American society, one that the conservative wing was still struggling to come to terms with.

"Paul, the production is almost at the wrap stage so I thought it would be a good time to let go a little and loosen up over a few drinks. There's a bar a short walk from here, and some of the others have said they will join us there later." Paul closed his laptop and followed Caitlin out of the office. At the bar, canapés were accompanied by beers. Caitlin knew that it would be at least an hour before the rest of the crew descended and disrupted their intimacy. "Paul, I like you and want to fuck you. How do you feel about that?"

"How I feel about that is it's a very no-holds-barred statement. This is weird, right? Where I come from women are not usually that forward. They will wait till after a few dates, at least, and even after a few drinks, that level of boldness is not expected. Caitlin, can I ask you something? Is this about race? Do you see me as an exotic import and you, perhaps, see yourself as the liberal white woman eager to show that diversity and inclusivity is part of her DNA? Do you want to fuck me because of what you think you know about me, a preconceived notion of black men, or do you want a relationship with me for who I am?"

"OK," said Caitlin. "It may have come across as a bit in your face, but I know people in the industry, and I know that you have ambitions to write scores for film and TV. I want to produce features and I thought that I could open a few doors for you. That's all. We'd make a good team. You're a hard worker, Paul, and good too."

"Yeah, by using my sexuality as a bargaining tool: you open a few doors for me while you, the successful producer, parade me around on your arm as your prize bull. Something doesn't sit right with me there, Caitlin. Yeah, I'm good. I know my shit when it comes to music, but my talent will get me where I want to go."

"Don't be naive Paul. I know people on the West Coast, and I will be heading to California as soon as possible. My friends in Hollywood tell me that there are some promising job opportunities in the pipeline, and I want you to come with me. I know you'd get where you want to with your music and writing but with my help, you could do it in half the time. Privilege has its benefits, you know. Besides, have you considered that I like you and it may not be about just sex. I like how you work; I like your intellect and how comfortable you are around others. There's a confidence there that I find attractive, and you have a great work ethic. This role play work scenario might look like a form of racism that is never talked about and acknowledged, but from my perspective, it really isn't. I know that race predicates everything in America, and while race might not carry such weight and history in the UK... I understand that class is the determinant factor in your society, right? The result is the same, right? I am told that where you come from, your class and status in society matters. Here, in the U.S., especially in our industry, I can open doors for you that will otherwise be slammed shut in your face - regardless of how talented and hardworking you are. You being a black man will only get you so far but in the end your ethnicity will get in the way. Hard work and talent alone aren't enough in the U.S. You will always be asking yourself if you could have done better, won more accolades, garnered more plaudits. And that is the reality of the situation. Yes, I might want to fuck you but there are certain benefits in Hollywood of being in a relationship with a white woman that you might not see now."

"So, I am not being used as a dildo substitute then?"

"Very wry. No, you are not being used in that way. My statement was bold because I was slightly irresolute, nervous. I saw how you and Andre get on and that you spend your weekends together clubbing and hanging out and I thought... well that you may have become very pally with him. Andre is a very sweet and likeable guy and a good man to have in charge of the lighting equipment, but he wouldn't be interested in me. I have the wrong bits to satisfy his preferences. But even if you are having sex with Andre, I am not judging. I have been divorced for four years now and if you don't count a smattering of disastrous online hook-ups, I have long forgotten what good sex is. It's all about work and career for me now. I married in haste, I don't want to repent at leisure, so my stated intent still stands, although the initial delivery could have been better presented."

Paul listened to Caitlin before responding: "To calm your nerves, I am not having sex with Andre. I like Andre, he's a great guy and has really looked after me since I have been here in New York, but I have someone back in the UK. She's waiting for me, although there are a few things we must sort out first. And I suppose the question is whether I want to fuck you. In my book it's not about the sex - I prefer to get to know someone first, then good loving follows. That might sound to your abrasive go-getting New Yorker's ear as quaint and cute, but it is just the way I am. If I have sex with you on your terms, I automatically assume the role of that like a dowager. After that, every job that comes my way, every opportunity that opens for me, I will be thinking that it's because of my manhood. It renders me impotent in a way that makes me very uncomfortable. I become helpless, defined by my gonads and nothing else. My talent immediately becomes invisible."

"The others are arriving now. Here's my address. I live in Long Island. It's Saturday tomorrow so bring a toothbrush. I'll be expecting you at about 9:30 this evening."

The evening flowed, the production team were happy that the long hours and the demands and the stresses of producing a television series was almost at an end. It was, indeed, time to relax. As Paul glanced at his watch, it was approaching 7pm. He calculated that if he took a taxi, he'd be at Caitlin's house by the appointed time. At the bar, he made his excuses and left, all the time conscious of Andre mapping his every step to the door. Andre could not hide his disappointment at Paul's early departure. He was hoping to invite Paul to accompany him as he showed off the city's underground haunts, the clubs and nightlife that was hidden from view. In his mind, an after-dark tour of secret Manhattan was going to be a prelude to what he had hoped would lead to something else. But Caitlin had beaten him to it.

As the taxi left Manhattan's familiar city skyline behind and headed down the freeway, a text flashed up on Paul's phone. "Tell the taxi to take the 25 and follow the signs to Massapequa." It was too late to change his mind. The farther away from Manhattan Paul travelled and the closer he got to Massapequa and Caitlin, the more his anxieties gripped his every thought. His last experience of being intimate with a woman ended badly. As Paul grappled with the prospect of intimacy with Caitlin, the thoughts of his clandestine liaisons with people of his own sex surfaced. "Men are so much easier when it comes to expressing their emotions. No ambiguity, no games... just simple. A few drinks and no-strings sex." He was determined not to give Caitlin more reasons to question his masculinity and he was determined to show her a strong, manly side, and not the part of his personality that would reveal his long struggle with his sexual orientation. As he pushed out the memories of his brimstone and fire preacher and the threatened eternal damnation of his youth, he found himself reciting the warnings of Leviticus 18:22, 20:13. The taxi approached Massapequa and Paul felt his heart rate increase and his hands becoming sweaty. He walked towards Caitlin's front door, strolling down a perfectly manicured lawn that was separated by a perfectly smooth path that meandered invitingly to her door. He pressed the bell. It opened to a smiling Caitlin who greeted Paul eagerly.

Caitlin was a vegetarian. Since she was a child, she could not understand why the human diet included eating animals, and much to the consternation of her parents, she was resolute in her determination to follow a plant-based diet. Yet, Paul was surprised at the smorgasbord of food that was on display - and none of it meat. Paul had not given much thought to not eating meat. Never had he had a reason to question whether or not it is right or healthy to consume animals as food. Caitlin explained that because of her dietary choices, she felt stronger, had more energy than her meat-eating peers and she was convinced that her plant-based diet was the reason why she was often mistaken for someone almost 10 years younger than her three decades. The food and the conversation made Paul feel relaxed. It eased his anxiety about any possible impending intimacy. However, Paul was not aware of how intimacy could trigger an episode of erotomaniac delusions relating to his sexual identity. The only reference that he had was Ellie. He could still not make sense of why their sexual encounter ended as abruptly as it began. He had questioned his actions and concluded that it somehow has something to do with his latent feelings for men over women. Feelings that he was determined to keep hidden from Caitlin.

"Are you ok Paul? You seem slightly ill at ease, tense even." Sensing that the evening was losing its flow, Caitlin let her hair down to relax her seemingly troubled guest. As her blonde tresses fell loose, covering Caitlin's shoulders, it had the opposite effect on Paul. To him it was a signal for closeness, intimacy. "More wine?" Caitlin offered. "Yes, thank you. It's a good red. Full-bodied and it goes down well. How long have you been a vegetarian? I ask because I cannot recall ever having a meal so delicious that does not contain meat of some kind. Usually, whenever I am confronted with a vegetarian meal, I find myself having to eat something soon after just to keep the hunger pains away. And why do you live so far away from where you work? The long commute must be tiring, right?" Paul was using conversation to avoid the inevitable conclusion of the evening, firing questions at Caitlin in a desperate attempt to keep the evening from spiralling into the inevitable. But it was becoming increasingly apparent to Paul that he was losing the battle of pushing back against Caitlin's lascivious intent.

"No, not at all. On this side of the Atlantic a two-hour daily journey to work is considered normal. Most of the people who work in Manhattan live upstate in places like Long Island or even Connecticut. I understand that in the UK, a two-hour commute to work would be frowned upon, people just wouldn't do it. Is that right?"

"Yes, no one travels to work longer than they must. Do you enjoy working in television? Silly question really, of course you do, that's obvious from what I see on set. Let me rephrase. Have you always wanted to be a producer?

"Yes, I have. Ever since I was little. I love telling stories and a good script sculpted in the correct way allows you to tell a good story. Have you brought condoms Paul?"

Caitlin's frank candour and skill at redirecting the conversation had again destabilised Paul's equilibrium, resulting in his sleeping demons being awakened. The non-threatening conversation had eased Paul's looming anxiety. He wanted the exchange of ideas and thoughts to continue, but the mention of condoms had ratcheted up his anxiety and brought to the surface the tangled prospect of sex and intimacy with a woman. He could not prevaricate any longer. "No, I hadn't... I did not think... I... Er! Sorry. I'm not used to sex on the first date so the thought of condoms had not occurred to me. Sorry! Sorry!"

"No need to be sorry, or to keep apologising. It's a good thing that I keep a fresh pack in my bedroom. Not that I am promiscuous, you understand. Far from it, but I don't take chances with my health, especially as New York has its fair share of bisexual men who get a thrill out of risky sexual behaviour. I don't see you as a risk. So, Paul, are you going to fuck me or not?" Paul felt like a rabbit caught in the headlights. He was a long way from the safety of his small, rented apartment in Manhattan and he felt exposed. He was fearful, even, that another woman would disappear after a night of lovemaking. When he was out on the town with Andre, he felt safe and while he knew that his co-worker was gay, Paul felt comfortable in the knowledge that Andre understood and respected Paul's personal boundaries, although Andre never properly understood what they were and could never pluck up the courage to ask Paul. Caitlin, on the other hand, was far from discreet. She was forceful, demanding and was not afraid to broach the difficult subjects head on. She was a woman who knew what she did and did not want and was not afraid to ask. Tonight, she wanted sex with Paul. She sensed that Paul was not as keen as she was for a night of what she hoped would be one of passion, but she was not overly concerned. In her mind any uncertainty about sex was Paul's problem, one that he had to come to terms with. She was, after all, doing him a favour in introducing him to her contacts in the film and television industry. Pleasuring her was a small price that he had to pay. It was his part of the arrangement that he had to deliver on.

Caitlin took Paul by the hand and led him to her bedroom. The spacious brightly decorated room had at its centre, a large bed that was beautifully adorned with expensive-looking sheets. Caitlin clearly had good taste. All Paul could see, though, was Ellie's small student digs. Caitlin allowed her flowing linen dress to fall slowly to the floor, revealing strong thighs and firm buttocks. Her positioning was deliberate. Caitlin would teasingly keep her round, full breasts and her pudendum hidden from Paul for as long as she dared. She enjoyed the sense of tease and the playfulness of her display of passion. All Paul saw, though, was Ellie. Caitlin instructed Paul to join her on the bed as she climbed under the sheets. He stood rooted to the spot. His memories of his night with Ellie had transfixed him. He could not move. Caitlin's carefully planned seduction routine had not gone as she had intended. The script had been torn up. "What is wrong? Is there something troubling you? Do you want to share what's on your mind, or would you rather just go to sleep? Look Paul, it's not a problem. We will have sex, it may not be tonight, but you will make love to me. But I don't want to put pressure on you."

Paul felt that he was not able to fight against the torrent of Caitlin's persuasiveness and slid under her welcoming sheets. In Paul's mind, having sex with a woman confirmed his masculinity, it removed the doubts and silenced his brimstone and fire preacher who assured damnation. Sensing his unease, Caitlin caressed Paul's firm nakedness, comforted him, and relaxed his tense muscles. The kisses were soft, and they settled into that practised interchange known to couples everywhere. But a familiar pattern soon emerged. First the slaps, then the pulling of hair. The aggression and intensity grew. The demarcation between lovemaking and assault became blurred. In the heat of the moment, Paul had become confused and discombobulated. Then it was over. "Wow, Paul. What the hell was that? I'm a physical kind of woman and can handle myself, but that was unexpected, rough in the extreme, borderline, even. That was not the kind of lovemaking I want or expect. And who the hell is Ellie, or Ella, you couldn't seem to make up your mind while you were pounding the life out of me." An increasingly confused Paul could not work out which way was up. He wanted to get away as fast as he could.

Paul barely closed his eyes as he lay silently beside a sleeping Caitlin. The hours ticked down and dawn's early glow seeped into the corners of Caitlin's bedroom. In the welcoming mottled light of the morning, it was clear that Caitlin had an eye for home decoration that was in keeping with her orderly life where every decision was planned, and nothing was left to chance. Every accessory was specifically chosen for its colour and how it complemented and joined together every decorative accent of her comfortable home. Paul glanced over to a still-sleeping Caitlin. He did not want to disturb her and stir her out of her deep sleep. Memories of the events of the previous evening had been pushed as far back into his thoughts as was possible: he did not want to relive what had happened; he certainly did not want to have a forced conversation with the woman sleeping on the bed that they had both shared. But Paul could not resist closing his eyes and imagining that the woman lying beside him was in fact Ellie. In his mind, Caitlin could have been Ellie. He imagined how things might have been if the circumstances had been different, if Ellie had not disappeared from his life so abruptly. He opened his eyes and looked at Caitlin's exposed flesh, the sheets ruffling down to reveal her naked back. The image of Caitlin - a mixture of sexiness and authority - made it difficult for Paul to resist the urge to reach for her, but he did resist and instead he edged slowly and carefully out of the bed and headed to the shower, collecting his clothes on the way. The hot water spurted out with a welcome force and Paul allowed himself to get lost in the rhythm of the shower, the water falling like a carefully constructed syncopated piece of music.

"Are you leaving without saying goodbye?" Paul, lost in his own musical creation, turned to see Caitlin staring at him inquisitively. "Yes, I must go. I didn't want to disturb you. You were fast asleep."

"Why? What's the hurry? You don't have to go anywhere. It's very early on a Saturday morning and we have to talk about last night."

"Er, yes, last night." The space between the en-suite shower and the bedroom suddenly appeared very small, engulfing Paul, trapping him. The bright, open, airy bathroom now felt claustrophobic. He felt cornered and looked around frantically to find a way out. But all exits were closing in around him. His gaze turned to the bedroom door that led to the hallway that led to the front door and freedom. But all Paul could hear were the words "we have to talk about last night". The seemingly innocent seven words swept him up and overwhelmed him. He didn't want to talk about last night. He wanted to run, to get away. At that moment he felt that he had been coerced into coming to Caitlin's house. He convinced himself that the situation that he now found himself in was her fault entirely because of her sexual manoeuvring. That she had forced him, bewitched him into making that long taxi journey to Massapequa only to entrap him. She had also forced him to have sex with her when he did not want to. Paul blinked because he wanted to change the narrative that was playing out in his mind, but instead he was taken back to that night at Ellie's small apartment all those years ago, but this wasn't Ellie, it was Caitlin whom he knew would demand answers to questions that he would not be able to respond to in a cognitive way. Enough time had lapsed between Ellie and where he now found himself, a passing of time that Paul had conceded to himself that he may have possibly given Ellie a reason not to want to see him again. But as he stood in Caitlin's bathroom, he knew that unlike Ellie, Caitlin would not shrink from a probing and frank conversation. A conversation that he was not prepared to have because he felt that it would mean having his worst fears held up in front of him by this strong, forceful woman. He had witnessed her authoritative control over the members of the film crew; he had seen, too, how she had a gentle but firm way of getting through to the people on the set, cutting away the masks and the prevarications. Caitlin was in charge and Paul did not want to take her on. Caitlin folded her arms across her chest, stood leant against the door frame of the bathroom and directed her full gaze on to the man she had just spent a night with. "Paul, look at me. Sex last night wasn't about sex, was it? There's so much more going on in your head than you're ready or willing to admit to. Am I right, Paul?"

"I must go Caitlin. Sorry." Paul dressed quickly without looking at Caitlin. He managed to evade her questioning as he made his way to her front door. But Caitlin wanted some answers before she would let him out of her sight. She moved swiftly and deftly, closing off his escape route. She was now at the front door. Arms framing her hips. Her inquisitive and intimidating stance stopped Paul in his tracks.

"You're not being honest with me, are you Paul? You are not telling me the whole story. You owe me an explanation. Something just doesn't add up and I want... no, I deserve answers. You don't just waltz into my home, fuck me, and think you can just waltz out again without giving an account of yourself as to why you suddenly went from Mr Nice to Mr Nasty once we were in bed together. Start talking. I am listening."

Paul knew at that moment that he had nowhere to run. He knew that he could no longer continue to hide behind the facade of the image of a red-blooded male. He knew, too, that he had to have that conversation with Caitlin, a conversation that would force him to confront his sexuality and his occasional secretive dalliances with men.

Caitlin was determined to find out what secrets Paul was keeping. "First, you need to explain to me why last night you kept calling me Ella and then Ellie and back again, interchanging each name as you went along your merry way. And for the record and in case you'd forgotten, my name is Caitlin. And then you can explain to me why you became so aggressive, so carnal, ditching any pretence of lovemaking for what to me was near-on full assault. It is entirely out of character for the person that I have come to know over these past months when we have worked together. That person did not resemble the person who was in my bed just a few hours ago. I am guessing that you are conflicted, tormented even. Paul, I am listening. Look, if it is what I am thinking, I am not averse to the soft touch of a woman myself so you're not the only one who has a hidden side."

Caitlin's own admission about occasionally waking up to the welcoming warm touch of a woman settled Paul, allowing him to open up to her. They talked and talked for hours, Caitlin teasing every drop of emotion out of

Paul. They talked until mid-morning, and Paul's uncertain disposition had retreated, the darkness within him being replaced by a liberating release as the conversation flowed between the two co-workers. Caitlin was a skilled communicator, able to listen, interjecting only when it was necessary, prodding and pushing Paul in the direction that he did not feel comfortable going. They talked until it was early afternoon. Paul explaining to Caitlin his tortured sexual dilemma that has been like an anvil around his neck for many years. Paul was spent. His head resting in Caitlin's lap, his eyes filling up with tears for what seemed like the umpteenth time. She cradled him and comforted him, drawing him closer to her with every sob. Paul had off-loaded a lifetime of confusion and uncertainty in one go. Caitlin proved to be the perfect sounding board, her compassion wearing down Paul's doubts and his stubborn refusal to acknowledge that it is ok to have feelings for men as well as women. Caitlin understood, too, how his resistance and refusal to embrace his sexuality would cause him to not want to expose himself to the judgement of his peers, his refusal to understand the complexities of his feelings for men when his community pushed him into believing that he could only have normal relationships with women. It also enabled him to address the pain within.

"Paul, you are not the world's first bi-sexual man - and you won't be the last. I get it that culturally it has been difficult for you to make sense of the contrasting feelings that you've had, and admitting to such things in some cultures is taboo, but keeping secrets will only tie you into knots, knots that can't always easily be undone if left alone. They just get more tangled. Paul, listen to me, everyone has skeletons in their closet; no one person's story is without an episode of soul-searching, of upset and rancour. Regardless of our race and our culture, we all have had at some point in our lives to deal with something we'd rather not face. The flipside of that, of course, is that there is also a welcome smile to counter the frown. I can help, if you want my help that is… and me wanting to help you has nothing to do with your manhood. Fundamentally, you are not a bad person, you don't intentionally hurt people, though Ellie and Ella might beg to differ. By the way, you owe both women a massive, huge apology.

Paul, you may not want to hear this but in my amateur evaluation, you show classic signs of schizophrenia. Are you Schizophrenic? The business that we are in is full of people who are functioning schizophrenics, or alcoholics, or gamblers, so you are not alone. We are born with a thousand different personalities. We slip in and out of each according to the needs of the occasion, but we die alone. As we go through life, we become who we choose to be. Think of it as a type of code switching. We change, we adapt, we stop, we go, we get so embroiled in the everyday that we lose track of who we really are. It's a symptom of modern life, Paul. Everyone has something to hide, but they manage to get on with their lives. If it is the case that you are suffering from Schizophrenia, it is a disorder that can be treated, Paul. Treatment enables the individual to see things in a different way, not the twisted representation of reality that can consume and bewilder, and a good, skilled therapist will see each person as an individual. There may be medication involved, Paul, but you will have to accept that you may be on antipsychotic medicines for a long time - maybe for a lifetime - and you will probably have to undergo some sort of cognitive behavioural therapy. But therapy is not a death sentence, Paul. People who suffer from some form of psychosis, including schizophrenia, do recover and live a normal life. I may be talking out of turn here, but I don't think that I am. You should consider therapy. It will help, I am sure. The fact that you opened up to me about the incidents in your past shows that you are willing and ready to make a change, to confront the things that have been controlling your behaviour and your choices. Time to heal, Paul. You are brilliant at what you do, you don't want to lose that, so you will have to learn to control your demons and your fears; and therapy enables you to do that."

Caitlin's words offered clarity. Suddenly, Paul could see things that existed outside his own mind, a mind that was previously filled with delusions. It was the first time that Paul had opened up about his true fears and feelings. With Caitlin's encouragement and support he was able to rationalise his erratic behaviour with logical reason. It was, he hoped, a new start that would allow him to put behind him those many moments of perplexity that had haunted him since he was a young adolescent. He lay in Caitlin's arms, the warmth of her words and the softness of her touch lulling him to sleep. At last, he felt safe.

Time Marches On

"Ray, have you completed the list of all the people that you want to invite to the wedding - and I mean everyone. I don't want a situation where two months later I hear spiteful gossip aimed at either of us because of this person or that person who wasn't invited. You know how vicious people can be, especially on social media, where anything goes, it seems."

"Ella, yes, of course I have invited everyone, I followed your instructions to the letter. Even Sgt King received his invitation. He assured me that we will finally meet the elusive Mrs Sgt King, his wife. In all the years that I have worked with him, I have never met her. Can you believe it?"

"I can believe it. And what about Paul? Have you heard from him? Does he even know that we are getting married? Do you think he would come to the wedding if you invited him despite all that has happened?"

"I don't know what has happened to Paul, Ella. I haven't spoken to him in about a year. In fact, after we found out about what happened between him and that girl at university, I have not set eyes on him, and I certainly haven't heard from him directly. And I am definitely not going to call him or go looking for him to invite him to our wedding. He's dead to me. You certainly haven't seen him; Michelle said her company no longer insures him so I have no idea where he might be. And frankly, I don't care. I don't want to hear any more talk about Paul. He's caused enough problems as it is. I did hear from your dad that he was doing well in New York working in television, writing scores and all that, but I also heard that he is back in London - or that he was for a while. Well, that's what I heard. One thing I do know, though, Ella, is that he won't be at our wedding".

"I thought I had asked you to leave Dad out of this. Dad will not take kindly to what he might have perceived as someone threatening me - or my brother or sister for that matter. Look, Ray, Dad tends to act on impulse. At work he is the epitome of diligence, he must be. But when it comes to his personal life, he does not suffer fools. I cannot imagine what he can do. When did you speak to Dad? I specifically asked you not to for this reason. Between his underworld contacts that he has met during his line of work, and the types of people that you know from your police work, it wouldn't be a stretch of the imagination to see the both of you conspiring to enact some sort of revenge on Paul, only, it won't be Dad or you who would be implicated. No! Neither of you would get your hands dirty. Am I right? It would be some poor sap who would be collared if Paul mysteriously came to some sort of harm. And why are you so certain that he won't be at the wedding? What have you and Dad done, Ray? I have said all along that despite how contemptible Paul's actions were towards me, he needs professional treatment, not a visit from a couple of heavies on a dark night in a dimly lit alley. In your masculine way, in trying to protect me, you and Dad have accomplished the opposite. Revenge is not a form of help, Ray. You know that I am against violence of any kind, even if Paul's vilification was directed at me. Now, I am not accusing you of anything, I just want to know that you've not done anything silly where Paul is concerned."

"Ok, ok, I did speak to your dad and we both agreed that we should not interfere with what happened to Paul. Yes, we both wanted to give him a good beating, and yes, Paul did come over as creepy and weird and dangerous, but we were concerned about you, I was concerned, and quite possibly Stephen was more concerned than most, despite your mother's advice, as sensible as it was, but we, that's your dad and me, agreed that common sense had left Paul a long time ago. It was time for action - and, believe me - the action we took was to agree to talk about it, which we did over a few beers. Nothing else. I know that Paul left the U.S. rather suddenly and your dad, using his position and influence as a successful criminal barrister, found out that he had a relationship with a co-worker that had ended rather abruptly. Does that sound familiar? He didn't know the details, but it meant that Paul had to make a quick exit and return to the UK. I don't know the circumstances either, but it sounds typical of Paul. I have not heard from him, nor have I seen him since he returned to the UK. I really don't know. He may even be back in America. And at this moment, I don't really give a shit."

"Which means Paul might be feeling all alone, abandoned by his so-called friends, which includes you, Ray."

"Why do you care about Paul's feelings after the way he treated that other woman and the twisted way in which he terrorised you because he couldn't separate reality from what was not real life. And who knows what happened in New York, maybe he was stalking one of his colleagues and turned nasty when he couldn't get his way. I know Paul. He can be as charming as the nicest person you could ever hope to meet, but he can also be the most twisted, vindictive individual you might ever come across. He's very clever and knows how to manipulate a situation or a person, for that matter, so that he gets his own way, yet he can be fragile and vulnerable in the next breath. There are two Pauls, one that needs to be punished, and yes, the other might well need some help."

"Actually, Ray, I do care. Regardless of what happened, Paul is still a human being, and a human being that needs help, not punishment."

"Who said anything about punishment?"

"You did. You implied there might have been an element of punishment. But don't you find it strange that he had to turn on his heels and leave New York as soon as he could? I'm going to call Dad."

"No, don't. I don't think we need to do that."

"We? I am going to call Dad. 'We' is plural, it means more than one, or is there something else that you're hiding from me, something that you and Dad haven't told me? Secrets that you are both keeping from me. Or maybe you have something to say to me first? Which is it, Ray? Have you ever thought that having Paul at the wedding might make him see that I am not his ex and that his relationship with her is a million miles away from who he might think I am in his messed-up way. Surely if he was there to witness us getting married, he would be able to see that his ex and I are two very different individuals?

"So, are you going to tell me what happened to Paul, or will I need to speak to Dad? Did you tell anyone at work what was happening, that Paul was stalking me, was making me feel as if I was imagining things, that I was beginning to question my sanity?"

"Yes, I mentioned it to a few of the lads, they were concerned about you, and yes, some of them thought that Paul needed a good seeing-to, a good going over, no questions asked, but I certainly didn't ask for any favours. And while we are being open and honest, you don't need to speak to your dad. We met, yes, and we thought about ways in which we could help, and we might have joked about calling in some favours from a few of his acquaintances that in the past he kept on the right side of the law, but it was nothing more than that. Your dad is very aware of your feelings about justice, and so am I, so nothing was decided other than that we would protect you in any way we could. He is aware, too, about your mother's opinion, that Paul needs professional help and not punishment. There was never ever any talk from either of us arranging for something bad to happen to Paul."

"OK, but you don't get it, do you? By talking to your mates and talking to my father, seeds were planted. They, the type of people you both know, may have felt that they would be doing you both a favour by taking things into their own hands. Unfortunately, Ray, you may have let the hounds out of the pen. You two are no better than our politicians who use language in a loose and lazy way. The only difference is that they do it deliberately to confuse and obfuscate. Freedom of speech is great, and a cornerstone of our democracy, and I am sure you and Dad didn't mean anything with your loose talk, but a suggestion, something implied, even in a casual, matey way, can have consequences. It's a red light to an opportunist. No one knows what happened to Paul, no one has seen or heard from him, and no one knows where he is. And more importantly, no one seems to be able to tell me what happened to Paul. That should concern you, Ray."

"I hear you Ella, but let's hope he patched up his differences with the woman that he was seeing in New York and returned there to continue with his ambition of writing musical scores. Can we drop the subject now? I don't think there's anything else to say on the matter, and I certainly don't think there's any mileage in speaking with your dad. He knows as much as I do."

"Yes, but what you both know is probably more than what you are both prepared to tell me. I am sure between you and Dad you know full well what happened to Paul, or at least where he is. But you won't tell me, and I understand that, I really do. But regardless of the messed-up way he treated me, it was not his fault, his actions were a symptom of his illness and not a result of clear intent. He may not have been my favourite person but there is a difference between someone who is cognisant and therefore in full control of his actions and carries them out in the full knowledge of what he is doing and someone who is ill and needs professional help, as Paul does. And for all we know, he probably still needs that professional help. What we will never know is if he ever received or is receiving the help that he needs."

"OK, OK. You win. I do know where Paul is. Your dad knows too. And I must apologise to you for holding back, but all your dad and I wanted was to protect you. Here's the truth. Paul is ok. He is in New York, where he is living, and he is also working some of his time in Hollywood where his work occasionally takes him. Your dad received an email from a woman by the name of Caitlin. Some of Stephen's legal contacts eventually managed to track him down, which is when Stephen received an email from Caitlin. I then received an email from Paul. For reasons best known to him, Paul felt that he owed me an explanation and an apology. Your dad shared the contents of Caitlin's email with me and that's how we know what Paul has been up to. Caitlin is obviously a trusted friend that Paul has made while he has been in America, and apparently, they worked together and indeed it was mentioned that they did have a relationship, albeit a short-lived one. However, Caitlin said she works with Paul, and she knows about what happened in his past. She mentioned in the email that Paul is in a better place now, and we've nothing to worry about. It seems your mum was right: he needed help, not punishment, and this woman seems to have been the catalyst for him to finally sort himself out. Caitlin said he is seeing a therapist and he is repentant about his past wrongs where you and Ellie are concerned. So now you know, and of course, this means that he won't be coming to our wedding. Look Ella, I'm sure Paul is doing fine. It's just the type of person he is. He's the kind of guy that always lands on his feet. So, can we leave it now? Please! Paul is Paul. He has the survival instincts of an alley cat. Look, we're getting married soon, so let's drop all this stuff about Paul. It's done. Over. He's living a new life in New York and Los Angeles. Let's focus on us. Agreed?"

Epilogue

Michelle shuffled her folder containing notes - plenty of them. She was prepared. "My lecture today will revolve around communication as an academic discipline and how language impacts on human communication and interaction, especially around interpersonal relationships in different social settings and different cultures and how language affects cultural identity." After an hour talking to her students, Michelle closed her laptop and turned to the undergraduates in front of her. "Yes, it's a big topic but as students in your second year of your degree course, I fully expect all of you to produce quality essays that dissects each aspect of what I have mentioned. And as a woman, and particularly a black woman, I have high standards, and as your new professor, I am particularly interested in what some of you will make of the cultural dimension of this discourse. I will start by turning the focus on to you by asking you to stretch your academic boundaries to their farthest limit and see how you get on. The question is this: what is cultural identity and how has it been interpreted and influenced by language, if at all? I am demanding, so I expect some quality work from this class."

It was Friday, the day before Ella and Ray's wedding, and Michelle was pleased with the way her first posting in her new position as a university professor was developing. It was a position that she had worked hard to get. She was rapidly climbing the ladder and reaching up to the glass ceiling with the fullest intention of smashing it into small pieces when she got there. It had been the best part of a year since Michelle had achieved her master's degree, and she was happy with her newly acquired position, happy with the direction in which her life was going, and happy that all the studying while working full time was behind her. And those tough times of balancing work with the demands of academia now seem a long-forgotten part of her journey. She was living her dream. "No more chasing difficult musicians over paperwork they have neither the desire for nor the knowledge of how to complete said paperwork," she thought to herself as she packed away her notes and packed away her laptop. She felt a glow of professional satisfaction that she had presented a clear and concise lecture, leaving the undergraduates equipped with enough knowledge and insight to go away and get their teeth into the topic that Michelle had set for them. Her thoughts turned to less demanding but no less gratifying considerations. It was the second week of a new term, Frankie was over from Spain for a long weekend, at the invitation of Ella who wanted to return the favour when she stayed in her flat in Oviedo. Yes, Michelle had every reason to be happy with her lot, she searched but could not find any reason as to why she would need to complain or feel out of sorts about how things had turned out for her. But this day wasn't her time to shine, the spotlight was on Ella and Ray.

At the wedding Michelle looked on, smiling at the happy, just-married couple as they walked down the aisle, Rebecca fussing over her big sister's dress. Michelle looked approvingly at Ray and reminisced to herself about the help he had given her on her road to becoming a university professor specialising in language. She smiled to herself at those early Sunday mornings and late weekday evenings when she'd knock on Ray's door and bombarded him with questions about language, class and race. She was also liking the fact that Rebecca had managed to talk her into not wearing black from head to toe to the wedding. "Too funerary, too depressingly goth," she remonstrated. Michelle had agreed on this one occasion to depart from her usual attire, convincing herself that blue is after all, just a few shades from black. Her tailored dress in a cadet blue with silver accents and matching shoes with carefully chosen jewellery that added a dazzling finishing touch was a departure for Michelle. She looked stunning and allowed herself a degree of contentment as she noticed the men sneaking an appreciative glance in her direction, and their women, clinging ever tighter to the arms of their beau, giving a not-so appreciative look in Michelle's direction.

"Rebecca, love does indeed conquer all, don't you think, including racial differences, prejudice, pre-held assumptions, history, convention, and class. Hatred and bigotry have finally been defeated, I am sure, and that multiculturalism is alive, just, at least it appears to be. It is still fighting for survival, despite the many challenges it faces," laughed Michelle. "Yes, love does conquer all," agreed Rebecca, hoping that one day, like her sister, she too would find her soulmate - as long as that person was not expecting her to compromise on her feminist views.

"And I am still wearing black, but you have to be extra nice to me if you want to see what's beneath this bodycon dress," Michelle quipped.

"You are a tease to the last, Michelle."

"Yes, she is - and she'll never change, that's why we love her," Frankie responded with a knowing grin.

Ella emerged from the church, clinging to her new husband as hard as she could, just in case something or someone would burst from the congregation and unexpectedly snatch him away from her with an impossibly convoluted reason. She was dressed in a slim-cut, figure-hugging shift wedding dress that mixed sobriety with the elegance of column sheath dress that she had persuaded the designer in the Greenwich shop to come up with. The dress, in an off-white embroidered pattern with sparkles, opaque butterflies and flowers sewn on top of a daring gossamer silk material, looked fantastic on Ella's tall, lean athletic figure that showed off her body's natural, willowy shape. Comfy flats in a subtle gold with a slight wedge at the heel were chosen ahead of high heels - Ella didn't want to be worrying about feeling uncomfortable on her special day; and heels were not usually her preferred choice of footwear. Ella shunned a vail on account of it being slightly old-fashioned, much to her mother's disappointment. Instead, her hair was adorned with flowers that matched those on her wedding dress. The understated necklace and bangle set off her attire to perfection, as did her delicately pretty corsage worn elegantly on her wrist.

Her mother and father, doing their parental duty for this one day only, carried it off in unison carefully avoiding spoiling the occasion with arguments from the past that had festered for years. Your daughter's wedding was not the time nor the place to dredge up almost-forgotten memories of indiscretions about the decisions that Ella's father made when she was a child. Even Sebastian was happy for his little sister - for once.

"Mrs Gordon," Ella whispered to herself with a grin that radiated. "Ray, some people are like clouds; when they're gone it's a beautiful day," Ella remarked as she snuggled into Ray's chest in the back of the silver convertible vintage car speeding them away from the church, on to the reception and the rest of their lives.

The End

Milton Keynes UK
Ingram Content Group UK Ltd.
UKHW020808080823
426520UK00017B/833